NEW DIRECTIONS FOR HIGHER EDUCATION

Martin Kramer
EDITOR-IN-CHIEF

How the Student Credit Hour Shapes Higher Education

The Tie That Binds

Jane V. Wellman
The Institute for Higher Education Policy

Thomas Ehrlich
The Carnegie Foundation for the Advancement of Teaching

EDITORS

Number 122, Summer 2003

JOSSEY-BASS
San Francisco

HOW THE STUDENT CREDIT HOUR SHAPES HIGHER EDUCATION: THE TIE THAT BINDS
Jane V. Wellman, Thomas Ehrlich (eds.)
New Directions for Higher Education, no. 122
Martin Kramer, Editor-in-Chief

Microfilm copies of issues and articles are available in 16mm and 35mm, as well as microfiche in 105mm, through University Microfilms Inc., 300 North Zeeb Road, Ann Arbor, Michigan 48106-1346.

ISSN 0271-0560   electronic ISSN 1536-0741

NEW DIRECTIONS FOR HIGHER EDUCATION is part of The Jossey-Bass Higher and Adult Education Series and is published quarterly by Wiley Subscription Services, Inc., a Wiley company, at Jossey-Bass, 989 Market Street, San Francisco, California 94103-1741. Periodicals postage paid at San Francisco, California, and at additional mailing offices. Postmaster: Send address changes to New Directions for Higher Education, Jossey-Bass, 989 Market Street, San Francisco, California 94103-1741.

New Directions for Higher Education is indexed in Current Index to Journals in Education (ERIC); Higher Education Abstracts.

SUBSCRIPTIONS cost $70 for individuals and $145 for institutions, agencies, and libraries. See ordering information page at end of book.

EDITORIAL CORRESPONDENCE should be sent to the Editor-in-Chief, Martin Kramer, 2807 Shasta Road, Berkeley, California 94708-2011.

Cover photograph and random dot by Richard Blair/Color & Light © 1990.

www.josseybass.com

CONTENTS

EDITORS' NOTES

Embedded in both the academic and administrative spheres, the student credit hour is truly the coin of the realm within higher education. This ubiquitous measure translates virtually all aspects of academic life into commonly understood public measures. The credit hour not only measures classroom time and student learning, it also is the basic measure for faculty workload; it provides the basis for calculating student "FTE-ness" (fulltime equivalence). This in turn becomes the building block for public funding, the foundation for most measures of institutional performance, and the basis for awarding degrees. The credit hour is the vehicle that allows students to transfer credits from one institution to another. It is a tool for translating the complex activities of diverse institutions into a common language, which (along with accreditation) knits together an otherwise diverse and diffused system of institutions of higher education. And it may be one of the biggest obstacles to institutional change because it perpetuates an accounting structure that was developed in the last century and may well have outlived its usefulness.

Higher education did not always have the student credit hour, and it still does not exist in most countries outside the United States, although it is coming in numerous nations, as shown in Chapter Eight. It has dual origins, one academic (the need at the turn of the twentieth century for standard measures of high school courses as the basis for college admissions) and the other administrative (the invention of foundations wanting to promote competition and productivity in higher education). Over the twentieth century, it had rapidly morphed into a public accounting device, a measure of workload that could be used to measure costs and efficiency in higher education. Now, more than a century later, the credit hour has a presence in every aspect of postsecondary policy: articulation between high school and college, student transfer, student-learning assessment and outcomes, content and integrity of the college degree, distribution of resources, and public accountability. Whether the credit hour actually defines and perpetuates some behaviors or simply shapes the way we talk about things, it has a powerful role.

The work described in this volume was begun because of a suspicion by the authors that the credit hour is an increasingly imperfect measure that may be causing or contributing to bad habits within higher education. These habits in turn may be getting in the way of improvements in teaching and institutional productivity tied to a more efficient use of resources to produce learning outcomes. The most obvious imperfections lie in its usefulness as a measure for student learning because time in the classroom is clearly no longer a sound basis for awarding academic credit to students, assuming it ever was. But the distortions between measure and purpose are not solely on the academic side. In fact, the measure of the credit hour is embedded in state and federal regulatory schemes for higher education, budget formulas, and accountability reporting. So even if a breakthrough in alternative ways occurs to measure student learning, the external administrative bureaucracy will continue to enforce standards based on a time-based measure.

With support from the Spencer, Hewlett, and Teachers Insurance and Annuity Association–College Retirement Equities Fund (TIAA-CREF) foundations, a research project designed to document the primary uses of the credit hour began, codirected by Thomas Ehrlich, of The Carnegie Foundation for the Advancement of Teaching, and Jane Wellman, at the Institute for Higher Education Policy. Our goal has been to document the ways the credit hour has come to be used and to inquire whether the measure perpetuates behaviors in higher education that get in the way of educational change. The work has been designed to investigate the following research hypotheses:

The credit hour is a barrier to innovation in teaching and learning.
The credit hour is a basic element of state budgets, and the measure gets in the way of budget reform.
The credit hour is more often enforced as a regulatory measure in public institutions than in private institutions and within the public sector in two-year institutions more often than in four-year institutions.
Innovative institutions work with and around the credit hour as a measure of student learning, but relatively few alternatives to the credit hour have occurred with respect to faculty workload.
Credit hours are awarded inconsistently, with little internal policy guidance or external review about the basis for awarding them.

Based on advice from an advisory committee (see the appendix at the end of the Editors' Notes) convened to help steer the work, we began by mapping the credit hour and identifying those aspects of its use that are most important from an educational policy perspective. To simplify the mapping, we distinguished between "internal" and "external" uses of the credit hour, as follows (see Table A).

Using the outline as a starting point, we explored the credit-hour regions that we and our advisors thought would be most fruitful. The chapters in this volume present the results of our explorations. It begins with the work of Jessica Shedd, who traces the development of the credit hour from its early days to the present. The results of an institutional survey of current policies and practices with respect to awarding credits for work are presented in Chapter Two. Thomas Ehrlich then considers whether the credit hour has been a barrier to institutional innovation through interviews with leaders of a dozen institutions widely believed to be innovators in higher

Table A. Credit Hour Uses in Postsecondary Education

"Internal" Institutional Uses	*"External"* Applications
Degree requirements, number of units required in general education versus in a major, etc.	U.S. Department of Education: Title IV Enrollments (credit hour is not reported but must be used to convert FTE and head count)
Measures of course credits recorded on transcripts	Clock or credit-hour requirements
Calculations of grade-point averages	Academic calendars
Faculty workload, compensation, and workload policies	Distance-learning (off-campus) status
Admissions requirements	Federal oversight of accreditors
Determination of enrollment status (full-time or part-time)	Review of academic progress
Residency requirements for degree attainment	Definitions of branch, off-campus, or correspondence teaching
Classroom assignments	Internal Revenue Service (eligibility for tax credits)
Staffing allocations	Interinstitutional student transfer
Financial reporting	State licensure requirements
Budget allocations	Rankings services (reporting)
Internal accountability reports	Accreditation standards for degrees, certificates, and diplomas
Building and space utilization standard	
Financial audits and program reviews	

education. The role of the credit hour as a measure of faculty work is then explored in another chapter by Ehrlich. Jane Wellman analyzes the administrative and regulatory uses of the credit hour in chapters that look at the role of accrediting agencies in enforcing it, state funding and the credit hour, and the federal government's enforcement of the measure. An analysis follows by Thomas Wolanin of some international dimensions of the credit hour. He examines how other countries that do not have the credit hour manage to cope without it. Finally, Chapter Nine summarizes what we have learned and presents some recommendations for the future.

Appendix: Members of the Advisory Committee

Lou Albert, Vice Chancellor, San Jose/Evergreen Community College District, San Jose, California

Judith Eaton, President, Council on Higher Education Accreditation, Washington, D.C.

Russ Edgerton, Director, Pew Forum on Undergraduate Learning, Washington, D.C.

Peter Ewell, Senior Associate, National Center for Higher Education Management Systems, Boulder, Colorado

Ann Ferren, Radford University, Radford, Virginia

Ruth Flower, Director, Government Relations, American Association of University Professors, Washington, D.C.

Merle Harris, President, Charter Oak State College, New Britain, Connecticut

Ronald J. Henry, Provost and Vice President of Academic Affairs, Atlanta
Dennis Jones, President, National Center for Higher Education Management
    Systems, Boulder, Colorado
Michael W. Kirst, Stanford School of Education, Stanford, California
Paul Lingenfelter, Executive Director, State Higher Education Executive
    Officers, Denver
Alex McCormick, Senior Scholar, Carnegie Foundation for the Advance-
    ment of Teaching, Menlo Park, California
Michael Middaugh, Assistant Vice President, Institutional Research and
    Planning, University of Delaware, Newark
Marianne Phelps, Consultant, Washington, D.C.
William Plater, Dean of the Faculties, Indiana University/Purdue University,
    Indianapolis
Linda J. Sax, Assistant Professor in Residence, Director, Cooperative Insti-
    tute Research Program, Associate Director, Higher Education Research,
    University of California, Los Angeles
Becky Timmons, Director of Governmental Relations, American Council on
    Education, Washington, D.C.

Jane V. Wellman
Thomas Ehrlich
Editors

JANE V. WELLMAN *is a senior associate with the Institute for Higher Education Policy in Washington, D.C.*

THOMAS EHRLICH *is a senior scholar at the Carnegie Foundation for the Advancement of Teaching.*

1

The student credit hour was invented as a tool for smoothing transitions from K–12 into higher education and was reinforced by foundations wanting to encourage business models—including competition and unit-cost analysis—in higher education.

The History of the Student Credit Hour

Jessica M. Shedd

How did the metric of the student credit hour come to be? It is not an organic, naturally occurring entity but is an invented artifice, intellectually derived to serve particular purposes. An American innovation, it was designed at the end of the nineteenth century to translate high school work to college admissions officers. It slowly made its way into higher education to record elective course work when standardized curricula began to erode. And it became widespread as the result of pressure from the philanthropic community interested in using business models to document workload and institutional productivity.

To document the evolution of the credit hour, we pieced together a picture derived from many sources. It included a standard review of the literature, a look at the history of The Carnegie Foundation for the Advancement of Teaching (central to the creation and expansion of the credit unit), the North Central Commission on Learning (the first regional accrediting commission to use the credit hour), the Association of American Colleges and Universities (currently researching the credit unit in relation to academic transfer), and several doctoral theses and unpublished papers.

Raubinger, Rowe, Piper, and West (1969) described the history of the credit unit as divided into three phases:

1873–1908: Increasing dissatisfaction with the college admissions process and high school-to-college articulation
1908–1910: The proposal and implementation of a standard high school unit

1910 to the present: The introduction of the Carnegie unit, its widespread growth, and its effect on both secondary and higher education

Gerhard (1955) breaks down the development of the credit system into two phases:

1870s and 1880s: With the rise of the elective system, colleges began to measure teaching in course and hour units.

Around the turn of the century: High schools and colleges assigned credit units to their courses and defined graduation requirements in terms of credits.

Additional stages and influences have guided the evolution of the credit hour into the broad-based measure that it is today. From its beginning as an academic measure of student learning for a rapidly growing student population, it has evolved into a measure of efficiency and faculty time and become a metric for internal budgeting and external data reporting. In general, three strands have coalesced to form the development of the credit hour: first, the need to handle enrollment growth and diversity while maintaining a handle on academic standards; second, desires from within higher education for curriculum reform and flexibility; and third, pressure from external stakeholders to force performance and accountability measures onto the educational establishment.

Phase I: College Admissions and a Standard High School Curriculum

From 1890 to 1900, the percentage of fourteen- to seventeen-year-olds going to high school almost doubled, and public high school enrollment continued to grow at an amazing rate into the early decades of the twentieth century (Lagemann, 1983). By 1910, more than 15 percent of fourteen- to seventeen-year-olds were enrolled in high school, a percentage that jumped to 32 percent by 1920. This was a period of enormous expansion for high schools, encouraging much discussion about the mission of the high school and its curriculum. This expansion made college possible for a greater number of students but also revealed a need for a standard measure of academic work completed in high school. National standards for high school programs and college entrance requirements became necessary not only to help high schools adequately prepare their students for college-level work but also to help colleges evaluate the increasingly large pool of applicants from a wide range of high school programs.

In the 1890s, the National Education Association appointed the Committee of Ten on Secondary School Studies, chaired by Charles Eliot from Harvard, and the Committee on College Requirements to address these issues (Levine, 1978). These groups prepared the reports that laid the groundwork for standardizing high school curricula across the country by designating programs with certain "unit" distributions as prerequisites to college acceptance. "Every subject which is taught at all in a secondary school should be taught in the same way and to the same extent to every pupil. Thus, for all pupils who study Latin, or history, or algebra, for example, the allotment of time and the method of instruction should be the same" (National Education Association, 1894, p. 17). The standard curriculum was to be provided to all students "regardless of their educational aspirations and that all subjects be held of equal rank for admission to college" (Levine, 1978, p. 159). Courses were to be calibrated in course units, which were based on contact-hour measures. Thus, learning was measured through time in class spent on the standard curriculum. The new system of measuring courses in units was designed to increase transferability of students and credits throughout the United States (Kreplin, 1971). The units were adopted by the newly formed College Entrance Examination Board of the Middle States and Maryland and by the North Central Association.

Development of the Carnegie Unit. Although The Carnegie Foundation for the Advancement of Teaching did not develop the idea of the unit, the foundation was instrumental in the widespread acceptance of the measure. In 1906, when the Carnegie Foundation was established, Andrew Carnegie gave $10 million to provide retirement pensions for college teachers. Concise definitions of college, university, professor, public versus private, and denominational versus independent institutions were needed, however, before a pension plan could be introduced. To "scientifically" define these terms, both the Carnegie Foundation and the General Education Board conducted extensive institutional surveys to formulate specific, empirical definitions for each term (Barrow, 1990). Drawing on the surveys and the State of New York's Regents Board standards for accreditation (Rudolph, 1977), the foundation proposed that a college be eligible for retirement allowances "if it (1) had at least six professors giving their entire time to college and university work, (2) had a course of four full years in liberal arts and sciences, and (3) required for admission not less than the usual 4 years of academic or high school preparation, in addition to the pre-academic or grammar school studies" (Raubinger, Rowe, Piper, and West, 1969, p. 81).

In addition, a college must accept the unit plan for admission, with a unit being defined as any one of four courses carried for five days a week during the secondary school year. Under ordinary circumstances, it assumed that a satisfactory year's work in any major subject cannot be accomplished in less than 120 sixty-minute hours or their equivalent. The "Carnegie unit," as it became known, was finally defined and accepted in 1909. The foundation explicitly stated that "in the counting the fundamental criterion was the amount of time spent on a subject, not the results attained" (Kreplin, 1971, p. 2).

The foundation also announced that if a college did not meet the requirements of the Carnegie Foundation's definition, it would not receive retirement allowances for its professors. Because few colleges at the time had their own pensions or annuity funds, the unit was quickly accepted in both colleges and high schools. By 1910 almost all high schools measured course work by the Carnegie unit (Raubinger, Rowe, Piper, and West, 1969).

Standardization and Measuring Efficiency. About the same time that the Carnegie unit was developed, the Carnegie Foundation and the General Education Board also supported the growing view that a fundamental problem with American higher education was that colleges were operating as separate units, leaving many institutions as "unguided and inefficient" providers of education (Barrow, 1990, p. 82). As a result, these organizations began to promote the idea of a single, standardized, and comprehensive system. The "scientific" definitions of *college* and *university* developed for the pension system provided a starting point by offering standard terms and definitions (Barrow, 1990).

In 1910, Morris L. Cooke published "Academic and Industrial Efficiency," a report that was underwritten by the Carnegie Foundation. The thinking of the time was that detailed "accounting and time-use" information that could be compared across time and between institutions was essential. The purpose of Cooke's report was to develop a formula to estimate the cost and output of both teaching and research—essentially "to measure the efficiency and productivity of educational institutions in a manner similar to that of industrial factories" (Barrow, 1990, p. 67). The goal of the work was to find a way to measure productivity in higher education to allow higher education to be subjected to competitive market pressures akin to those in private industry. To accomplish this, Cooke developed a "calculus" with a key unit of measure called the *student hour,* defined as "one hour of lectures, of lab work, or recitation room work, for a single pupil" (Barrow, 1990, p. 70). This measure made possible the calculation of relative faculty workloads, the cost of instruction per student hour, and ultimately, the rate of educational efficiency for individual professors, fields, departments, and universities. As a result of Cooke's report, the Carnegie Foundation published "Standard Forms for Financial Reports," which required standard administrative and accounting forms and procedures for all colleges applying for the Carnegie Foundation pension system.

Throughout the next decade, public higher education was redefined as a "social investment" in the economy. Public institutions, forced to justify their "rate of return" to the public, began to survey themselves to obtain data such as cost per student hour. Efficiency surveys thus became increasingly popular, and Cooke's "student hour" was adopted as the basic measure of production. By the end of the 1920s, institutional data recording and retrieval systems had been restructured to accommodate nationally standardized measurements of productivity and rates of return on investment (Barrow, 1990).

The Elective System. In his 1869 inaugural speech as president of Harvard University, Charles W. Eliot (who also chaired the board of trustees at the Carnegie Foundation) made public his commitment to the elective system. Eliot saw electives as a motivator for students and a way for them to study the subjects in which they were naturally talented or interested. By 1872, all subject requirements for seniors at Harvard were abolished, and by 1885, requirements even for freshmen were reduced. The change from a standard curriculum to the elective system fundamentally altered the content of the college degree from something awarded based on the mastery of a comprehensive curriculum to the successful completion of a series of courses. With this curricular change, however, colleges needed a way to keep track of courses and students' progress along the various paths toward their degrees. Determining how course work should be measured and progress to the degree monitored constituted the major challenge in implementing the elective system.

The first units of measure were the courses themselves, which were defined in hours of classroom contact. By 1877, the University of Michigan catalogue indicated that twenty-four or twenty-six full courses were required for the bachelor's degree and that a full course equals "5 exercises a week during a semester, whether in recitations, laboratory work, or lectures" (Gerhard, 1955, p. 654). The measure of achievement was based on a common time unit, and the accumulation of the set courses and time units constituted a complete bachelor's-level education.

The larger state universities in the Midwest and West were the most eager to adopt the elective system, whereas the least receptive schools were the smaller, private New England colleges. By the 1890s, however, the universities of Wisconsin and Michigan were among the few major institutions that still maintained required freshman and sophomore courses. Over time, the expanded choices that the elective system provided led to the creation of majors and minors, academic departments, and specialization of scholarship (Lucas, 1994).

The growth of the elective system was related to the spread of mass secondary education. Public opinion called for a wider variety of college courses more appropriate to the diverse interests of high school graduates. Demand to make institutions more attractive to the broader public led to a huge increase in course titles and a corresponding need for some way to document students' progress. With a greater number entering higher education, student mobility also increased and quantitative, transferable learning units became critically important.

Phase II: Administrative, Budgetary, and Regulatory Enforcement

Once the basic credit-hour measure had developed, its use as an administrative, reporting, and external monitoring device began to evolve. The companion background articles in this project go into greater detail about all of these elements. In brief, the following are some of the major themes affecting this evolution.

Federal Financial Aid and Regulation of Higher Education. The federal role in higher education expanded enormously as a result of the enactment of the GI Bill. Research on the GI Bill has shown that concern about quality and "diploma mills" led the federal government to require that institutions be accredited to be eligible for GI tuition reimbursement. For many years, the federal government deferred to the accrediting agencies to make judgments about academic quality. This deference was eroded considerably with the growth of Title IV student aid programs in the 1980s and 1990s and the perception of problems of fraud and abuse in these programs. As a result, the federal government intensified its oversight of accrediting agencies through a federal "recognition" process—the federal regulation of accrediting agencies seeking to be "gatekeepers" for Title IV funds. Accrediting agency standards and procedures that previously were internal to the agencies began to leach into federal law as standards for federal review and recognition of accrediting agencies. At the same time, the federal government began to import standards such as the credit hour into its own requirements for institutional eligibility for Title IV and for record keeping. In addition to requiring the institutions to measure learning either through credits or "clock hours," the government required institutions to maintain standard academic calendars built on credit or clock hours. These measures became standardized and enforced through the regulation of institutional eligibility to receive Title IV funding.

Data Reporting. Federal government research has reinforced the use of the credit-hour measure in higher education. The credit-hour measure has been embedded in federal data systems since the 1960s. Integrated Postsecondary Education Data Surveys is one such system that relies on the measure. Federal systems are in turn the basis for most public information about higher education, such as the Common Data System used by the rankings agencies. All states have also standardized their data collection formats to conform to federal information requirements.

State Budgeting Systems. The credit hour came into widespread use as the basis for formula budgets for public institutions of higher education somewhere in the 1960s, probably as a result of the expansion of public, multicampus systems that occurred during this time. This was also the era of "PPBS"—program-planning budgeting systems—throughout state government. In several states, formula budgets based on enrollment-generated credit hours became the building block for the distribution of public funds. As one example, the history of the University of California system shows that what was then called "performance-based" budgeting based on the credit hour was one of the early reforms instituted under Clark Kerr's leadership as president of the Berkeley campus, when the "system" moved from a Berkeley-flagship model to the "multiversity" (Douglass, 2000).

Collective Bargaining. The rise of faculty collective bargaining in public higher education has likely been another force for cementing the use of the credit hour as a measure of faculty classroom contact. (For more on this subject, please refer to the companion background chapter [Chapter Four] by Thomas Ehrlich on collective bargaining and faculty workload.)

Phase III: Present and Future: The "Deinstitutionalization" of Higher Education

Students today are increasingly obtaining access to higher education through lifelong learning, multiple student transfers, and off-campus or distance learning. Students are increasingly disloyal to individual institutions and accumulate courses toward a degree from several institutions. According to a study conducted by Adelman (1999), over 60 percent of undergraduates attend more than one institution, and 40 percent transfer across state lines. Student mobility has taken on a new meaning because of educational technology and distance learning, which has allowed courses to be made portable through the World Wide Web. Some institutions of higher education, such as Charter Oak State College (described in more detail in Chapter Three), award degrees based on assessments of student course portfolios from multiple institutions. In this model, the institutional role has changed into one of assessment of course work rather than direct provider of instruction or guardian of the curriculum.

Frustrations with the inadequacies of the credit-hour measure—its inattention to student learning and its time-and-location-based method for recording learning—are particularly evident in the areas of transfer and distance education. This is true despite the fact that the credit hour is the vehicle that allows student learning to be recorded and transferred across many types of institutions. Distance education, in particular, is exerting pressure on the traditional measures of learning—because it forces a review of institutional policy on issues such as contact-hour requirements, budgeting structures, and infrastructure (Twigg, 1999). Even the federal government, in an attempt to respond to pressures from "virtual institutions," has adapted slightly in granting waivers to some of the Title IV fund eligibility regulations. For example, the "50-percent rule," which requires a minimum of 50 percent of an institution's courses to be taught on campus, has been waived to accommodate many distance education-based institutions (for more on this subject, please refer to Chapter Six by Jane Wellman on federal regulations).

Conclusions

Although the student credit hour's origins are rooted in events that occurred over a century ago, the themes surrounding its creation and use have not fundamentally changed. In fact, this exploration of the evolution of the credit hour has a déjà vu quality to it. Virtually all of the major issues that shaped the evolution of the measure are alive today: the explosion of enrollments, the desire to ensure that all students learn to a common standard, the need to correlate high school graduation requirements with college admission standards, pressures for public accountability, desires for greater institutional efficiency and productivity, student transfer and mobility, and attention to the quality and integrity of the collegiate curriculum. Developed in an industrial era well before the massification of higher education, the measure itself has remained essentially unchanged. Whether that is attributable to its adaptability or a sign of the basic calcification of higher education remains an open question.

References

Adelman, C. *Answers in the Tool Box: Academic Intensity, Attendance Patterns, and Bachelor's Degree Attainment.* Washington, D.C.: Office of Educational Research and Improvement, U.S. Department of Education, 1999.

Barrow, C. W. *Universities and the Capitalist State: Corporate Liberalism and the Reconstruction of American Higher Education, 1894–1928.* Madison: University of Wisconsin Press, 1990.

Cooke, M. L. *Academic and Industrial Efficiency: A Report to the Carnegie Foundation for the Advancement of Teaching.* New York: Carnegie Foundation for the Advancement of Teaching, 1910.

Douglass, J. A. "A Tale of Two Universities of California: A Tour of Strategic Issues Past and Prospective." *Chronicle of the University of California,* Fall 2000, pp. 93–118.

Gerhard, D. "The Emergence of the Credit System in American Education Considered as a Problem of Social and Intellectual History." *AAUP [American Association of University Professors] Bulletin,* 1955, *41,* 647–668.

Kreplin, H. *Credit by Examination: A Review and Analysis of the Literature.* Berkeley: Foundation Program for Research in University Administration, University of California, 1971.

Lagemann, E. C. *Private Power for the Public Good: A History of the Carnegie Foundation for the Advancement of Teaching.* Middletown, Conn.: Wesleyan University Press, 1983.

Levine, A. *Handbook on Undergraduate Curriculum.* San Francisco: Jossey-Bass, 1978.

Lucas, C. J. *American Higher Education: A History.* New York: St. Martin's Griffin, 1994.

National Education Association. *Report of the Committee of Ten on Secondary School Studies, with the Reports of the Conferences Arranged by the Committee.* New York: American Book Company, 1894.

Raubinger, F. M., Rowe, H. G., Piper, D. L., and West, C. K. "*The Development of Secondary Education.* Old Tappan, N.J.: Macmillan, 1969.

Rudolph, F. *Curriculum: A History of the American Undergraduate Course of Study Since 1636.* San Francisco: Jossey-Bass, 1977.

Twigg, C. A. *Improving Learning and Reducing Costs: Redesigning Large-Enrollment Courses.* Troy, N.Y.: Center for Academic Transformation, Rensselaer Polytechnic Institute, 1999.

JESSICA M. SHEDD is a research analyst in the Office of Institutional Research and Planning at the University of Maryland, College Park.

2

Although all institutions use the student credit hour, it is rarely defined and not consistently enforced.

Policies and Practices in Enforcing the Credit Hour

Jessica M. Shedd

This chapter describes the results of an institutional survey designed to learn how different colleges and universities apply the credit hour—whether they use it to measure credits to graduation, how they define it, and how they determine the number of credits to award for any course. We also did a survey of credits in relation to time in class—that is, the extent to which these institutions continue to use time as one of the primary bases for awarding credits.

Working with the Office of Institutional Research at the University of Delaware (UD/OIR), we invited about seventy-five institutions to participate in a survey of their policies and practices with regard to awarding the credit hour. The institutions were drawn from participants in the past six years of a survey administered by the University of Delaware on instructional costs.

Institutions were identified by the UD/OIR based on their participation in the instructional cost survey and their reputation for having "good" data management. Participation was voluntary, and the anonymity of the participating institutions preserved. The survey consisted of two parts: one, a request for information about their written policies and procedures for assigning credits to classroom time, and two, an analysis of course data files to evaluate the relation of classroom time to credits awarded. Of the seventy-five institutions invited, fifty-five agreed to participate in providing a course data file, as follows:

- Forty-two public and thirteen private institutions
- Nineteen research or doctoral institutions

NEW DIRECTIONS FOR HIGHER EDUCATION, no. 122, Summer 2003 © Wiley Periodicals, Inc.

- Seventeen master's or comprehensive institutions
- Ten baccalaureate institutions
- Nine associate of arts (community college) institutions (all public)

Thirty-eight institutions returned the request for information about their written policies and procedures related to the credit hour (sixteen from research or doctoral institutions; sixteen from master's, comprehensive, or baccalaureate institutions; and six from associate of arts institutions). Despite underrepresentation from private institutions (with respect to the number of institutions nationally), the final mix constitutes a healthy sampling of institutional types. The small number of private institutions and the small number of courses in the private institutions also mean that we did not try to distinguish between public and private institutions in the analysis of discipline and course level, although we present the data on course modalities separately for the private institutions. The results are not statistically representative and cannot be generalized to all of higher education.

Policy Survey Results

The policy survey was designed to provide background information on internal institutional policies and practices for the credit hour. We asked the institutions to tell us the following:

The predominant way that the institution records student learning or course work (credit hour, courses, or other)
Whether their course catalogue or faculty handbook includes a specific definition of a credit unit
Whether their state codes or regulations define the student credit unit
Whether the course catalogues provide students with guidelines about expected out-of-class study time in relation to class time
Whether the institution maintains written policies or guidelines for determining the number of credits a new course should be worth
Whether the faculty workload policies refer to class hours, course hours, or other measures of classroom teaching time
What their academic calendars are (semester, quarter, or other)

The results of this survey are presented for both two- and four-year institutions in Table 2.1. The results show the following:

Almost all (36 [95 percent]) responding institutions use the credit hour as the predominant means of recording student learning. This figure was lower for two-year colleges—five (83 percent) two-year institutions use the credit hour whereas one (17 percent) reports using the number of courses as their predominant means of recording learning.

Table 2.1. Policy Survey Results (number [percentage]) by Type of Institution

Please indicate the predominant way that your institution records student learning or course work.

	Credit Hour	Courses	Other
All institutions (n=38)	36 (95)	1 (3)	1 (3)
Research (n=16)	100	0	0
Comprehensive or baccalaureate (n=16)	15 (94)	0	1 (6)
Associate (n=6)	5 (83)	1 (17)	0

Does your course catalogue or faculty handbook include a specific definition of a credit unit?

	Yes	No
All institutions	16 (42)	21 (55)
Research	6 (38)	9 (56)
Comprehensive or baccalaureate	6 (38)	10 (63)
Associate	4 (67)	2 (33)

Do your state codes or regulations define the credit hour?

	Yes	No	Other Agency	Don't Know
All institutions	10 (28)	12 (33)	1 (3)	10 (28)
Research	2 (13)	5 (36)	0	6 (40)
Comprehensive or baccalaureate	3 (20)	7 (47)	0	4 (27)
Associate	5 (83)	0	1 (17)	0

Does your course catalogue provide students with guidelines about expected out-of-class study time in relation to class time?

	Yes	No
All institutions	4 (11)	34 (90)
Research	3 (19)	13 (81)
Comprehensive or baccalaureate	0	16 (100)
Associate	1 (17)	5 (83)

Does your institution maintain written policies or guidelines for determining the number of credits a new course should be worth?

	Yes	No
All institutions	14 (38)	23 (62)
Research	6 (40)	9 (608)
Comprehensive or baccalaureate	4 (25)	12 (75)
Associate	4 (67)	2 (33)

Do your faculty workload policies refer to class hours, course hours, or other measures of classroom teaching time?

	Yes	No	Varies by Department
All institutions	27 (73)	7 (19)	3 (8)
Research	7 (47)	5 (33)	3 (20)
Comprehensive or baccalaureate	15 (92)	2 (6)	0
Associate	8 or 7 (89 or 78)	1 or 2 (11 or 22)	0

What is your institution's academic calendar?

	Semester	Quarter	Other
All institutions	33 (87)	3 (8)	2 (5)
Research	15 (94)	1 (6)	0
Comprehensive or baccalaureate	14 (88)	0	2 (13)
Associate	4 (67)	2 (33)	0

A solid majority (twenty-seven [73 percent]) of responding institutions indicated that their faculty workload policies refer to class or course hours, although there was variation between research or doctoral institutions (only seven [47 percent]), as compared with fifteen (94 percent) master's and baccalaureate institutions and five (83 percent) associate of arts colleges.

Although institutions use the measure to record learning and faculty workload, most do not define the term for students or faculty: of the institutions responding, twenty-one (55 percent) do not define credit units in either their course catalogue or faculty handbook. The absence of definition or internal policies for credits is particularly pronounced among the thirteen private institutions in this survey, of which only four (31 percent) included a definition of the credit unit in their course catalogue or faculty handbook. Interestingly, the results are a little different for two-year institutions: four of the institutions (67 percent) responding include a definition of the credit unit in their course catalogue or faculty handbook. In addition, about 90 percent ($n = 34$) of the institutions reported that they do not have formal written guidelines for students specifying expectations for out-of-class study time.

Only ten institutions (28 percent) reported that their state codes or regulations define the credit hour, twelve (33 percent) answered that their state codes did not define the credit hour, and ten institutions (28 percent) did not know what the state regulations said.

In most four-year institutions, there are no written policies or guidelines clarifying the basis for determining how credits should be assigned to new courses. Only fourteen of all responding institutions (38 percent) and ten four-year institutions (31 percent) have such policies. In contrast, two-thirds ($n = 4$) of the two-year colleges report that they have such guidelines.

Methods and Data Collection Process for the Analysis of the Course Record Files

The course file data from two- and four-year institutions were studied separately. The data files were analyzed for patterns in the awarding of course credit with respect to time spent in class by Carnegie classification, type or control of the institutions (only for four-year institutions), course levels (only for four-year institutions), and Classification of Instructional Programs (CIP) code or discipline of the courses (National Center for Education Statistics, 2002). To maintain the integrity of the data sets and to ensure that the data analyzed were best suited to the purposes of this study, several actions were taken. Records were eliminated at each step of the following "data-cleaning" process (Table 2.2).

Only courses with scheduled class times provided in the files could be included in the analysis. Without this information, contact hours or time

Table 2.2. Number of Course Records Eliminated from the Analysis at Each Stage of the Data-Cleaning Process

Stage of Elimination	Four-Year Institutions	Two-Year Institutions
All courses analyzed		
Total (before elimination)	62,828	15,019
Invalid meeting time	10,392	2,572
CIP code (missing or too few)	1,193	319
Variable credit course	2,930	114
Class meeting time >10 hr	272	276
Course credit >6 credits	136	19
Total remaining	47,905	11,749
Lecture courses		
Total (before elimination)	44,812	9,395
Invalid meeting time	7,113	1,659
CIP code (missing or too few)	909	156
Variable credit course	1,370	98
Class meeting time >10 hr	61	49
Course credit >6 credits	115	12
Total remaining	35,244	7,421
Lecture courses with lab or discussion		
Total (before elimination)	8,516	4,851
Invalid meeting time	715	610
CIP code (missing or too few)	158	120
Variable credit course	662	12
Class meeting time >10 hr	166	207
Course credit >6 credits	11	7
Total remaining	6,804	3,895
Nonlecture courses		
Total (before elimination)	9,500	773
Invalid meeting time	2,564	303
CIP code (missing or too few)	126	13
Variable credit course	898	4
Class meeting time >10 hr	45	20
Course credit >6 credits	10	0
Total remaining	5,857	433

Note: Numbers in tables throughout the chapter are less than 3,895 because courses with CIP codes 47, 48, and 49 (mechanics and repairers, precision production trades, and transportation and materials moving workers, respectively) were excluded because of small sample sizes and concern about the quality of the data in these areas.

spent in class could not be calculated. Unfortunately, a substantial number of courses in these files had class times listed as "to be announced." These "nonorganized courses" would include most independent study courses or other courses of this nature, where the terms of the course are agreed on between the sponsoring faculty member and the student.

Only course records with a CIP code (National Center for Education Statistics, 2002) listed in the file were included. The CIP code is essential for analyzing by discipline.

Only fixed-credit courses were included in the analysis because it is not possible, with the information we were provided, to determine the relationship between credits awarded and time spent in class from a variable credit course.

Only courses with class meeting times of less than ten hours a week were included. It is not possible to check the accuracy of the scheduled time in the course file, and because classes longer than ten hours a week were rare, this information was likely an error in the file, and these classes were removed from the analysis to prevent improper skewing of the data.

Only courses worth one to six credits were included in the final analysis. Because a minimal number of courses were worth more than six credits, they were eliminated from the analysis to ensure that they would not skew the analysis and results.

Courses were categorized into lectures, lectures with labs or discussion sections, and nonlectures. The courses not falling into one of these three categories were the "nonorganized courses" discussed above, most of which did not list a course time. For this reason, these courses had to be eliminated from the analysis.

Whenever possible, labs or discussion sections listed separate from the lecture they were associated with were joined with the appropriate lecture. They were then summarized together into one record.

The quality of the data and the small number of institutions participating in the survey clearly limit the extent to which the study results can be generalized across all of higher education. The research or doctoral institutions had the most course records, by far, which could skew the results toward patterns in these institutions. The most important aspect of the data quality is that courses without an organized time or credit worth listed could not be analyzed. Most courses without time or credit listed were nonorganized courses such as independent studies or research, clinical instructions, and the like. As a result, courses that may most likely be less traditional in their credit worth and schedule time are not included in the analysis (Table 2.3). This issue primarily affects the analysis in four-year institutions, where these nonorganized courses comprise a much larger percentage of total reported courses than they do in the two-year institutions.

Table 2.3. Total Reported Courses by Course Type and Type of Institution Before Data-Cleaning Process

Type of Course	Four-Year, no. (%)	Two-Year, no. (%)
Lecture	44,812 (55.7)	9,395 (60.3)
Lecture with lab or discussion	8,516 (10.6)	4,851 (31.2)
Nonlecture	9,500 (11.8)	773 (5.0)
Nonorganized	17,602 (21.9)	553 (3.6)
Total	80,430	15,572

Note: Numbers in parentheses are percentages.

Course File Data Results for Four-Year Institutions

Each course analyzed was designated as either a lecture, lecture with a lab or discussion, or a nonlecture course. Overall, 74 percent of the courses suitable for analysis were lectures, 14 percent were lectures with a lab or discussion component, and 12 percent of the courses were considered non-lecture courses. Courses overwhelmingly fall into the traditional three-credit lecture course—73 percent of lectures are listed as three-credit courses. The lecture courses with labs or discussion components are concentrated in three- or four-credit courses whereas nonlecture courses are concentrated in one- or three-credit courses (Table 2.4).

The overall patterns in course offerings are true for the research or doctoral and the master's or comprehensive institutions, but the baccalaureate institutions in the study at times differed from the overall trend. These institutions offered most of their lecture courses for four credits, and their nonlecture courses were more evenly distributed across course worth than in the other types of institutions.

Class or Course Hours. The survey results suggest that the use of time is more uniform than practices for awarding credit in relation to time: lecture courses seem to meet an average of three hours a week regardless of the credit they are worth. However, within lecture courses, the most variation seems to occur in average class hours per week in the research or doctoral institutions. The mean class hours per week at research or doctoral

Table 2.4. Number of Courses by Course Credit, Course Type, and Institution Carnegie Classification, Four-Year Institutions

	Course Credit					
Institutional Type	1	2	3	4	5	6
Lecture						
All institutions	2,664	1,505	25,712	4,734	371	258
Research	2,013	890	17,936	2,382	260	197
Comprehensive	601	518	7,379	835	75	42
Baccalaureate	50	97	397	1,517	36	—
Lecture with lab or discussion						
All institutions	334	542	3,526	2,212	137	53
Research	237	327	2,750	1,835	131	49
Comprehensive	83	182	664	118	—	—
Baccalaureate	—	33	112	259	—	—
Nonlecture						
All institutions	2,588	677	2,136	366	55	35
Research	2,011	219	1,278	95	—	—
Comprehensive	518	377	798	152	—	—
Baccalaureate	59	81	60	119	—	—

Note: In the rest of the tables in this chapter (Tables 2.5 through 2.18), a dash indicates $n < 30$ This was considered to be too few course records to include in the analysis and on which to base conclusions.

institutions ranged from 2.17 hours for one-credit courses to 4.15 hours for the six-credit courses (Table 2.5).

There was more variation in meeting time for course credit in lecture courses with a lab or discussion component than with the pure lecture courses. The lecture courses with labs and discussion components tended to meet between four and five hours a week regardless of the credit they are worth. Still, the lack of variation overall between time spent in class is surprising; three hours is clearly standard for a lecture course, and four or five credits appears to be standard for a lecture with a lab or discussion component regardless of how much credit will be earned for the course.

Patterns for Public Versus Private Institutions. In the public institutions, the lecture courses are highly concentrated in three-credit courses, and the private institutions' lecture courses are almost evenly concentrated in three- and four-credit courses (Table 2.6). Private institutions may deviate from the three-credit lecture norm more than the public institutions. No major differences were apparent between the public and private institutions with lecture courses with labs and discussions and nonlecture courses; the overall trends hold for both types of institutions.

The only noticeable difference in mean time spent in class was that on average, the lecture courses with lab and discussion components met for a longer time in public than in private institutions (Table 2.7).

Patterns by Course Level and Discipline. The patterns by course level do not appear to be different from the overall trends discussed above.

Table 2.5. Mean Scheduled Time in Classroom per Week by Course Credit, Course Type, and Institution Carnegie Classification, Four-Year Institutions

Institutional Type	Course Credit					
	1	2	3	4	5	6
Lecture						
All institutions	2.26	2.67	2.92	3.16	3.36	3.84
Research	2.17	2.71	2.95	3.39	3.66	4.15
Comprehensive	2.56	2.62	2.86	2.96	2.64	2.77
Baccalaureate	2.14	2.64	2.72	2.91	2.68	—
Lecture with lab or discussion						
All institutions	4.39	4.15	4.60	5.11	5.20	5.09
Research	4.54	3.99	4.61	5.21	5.20	5.25
Comprehensive	4.10	4.45	4.56	5.41	—	—
Baccalaureate	—	4.03	4.38	4.25	—	—
Nonlecture						
All institutions	2.41	2.71	3.34	3.41	3.34	4.07
Research	2.39	3.64	3.54	3.20	—	—
Comprehensive	2.44	2.06	3.03	3.87	—	—
Baccalaureate	2.72	3.17	3.32	3.00	—	—

Note: See Table 2.4 footnote for explanation of the dashes.

Table 2.6. Number of Courses by Course Credit, Institutional Control, and Course Type, Four-Year Institutions

Institutional Control	Course Credit					
	1	2	3	4	5	6
Lecture						
Public	2,173	1,183	21,098	2,230	288	181
Private	284	255	2,736	2,146	82	77
Lecture with lab or discussion						
Public	280	503	2,768	1,459	103	39
Private	49	31	419	437	34	—
Nonlecture						
Public	2,096	516	1,636	215	52	—
Private	357	83	468	133	—	—

Note: See Table 2.4 footnote for explanation of the dashes.

Regardless of the level of the course, the three-credit lecture still appears to be the most prevalent mode of instruction (Table 2.8). One point of interest may be that a high number of nonlectures for the lower-division undergraduate courses appear to be one credit. Finally, patterns in mean scheduled class time do not seem to differ from those overall (Table 2.9). Unfortunately, where different trends may occur, the numbers are small, and any conclusions or generalizations are inappropriate.

Patterns between disciplines in the assignment of credits to class time do not appear to be strikingly different (Tables 2.10 through 2.13). However, for lecture courses with lab or discussion components, the

Table 2.7. Mean Scheduled Time in Class per Week by Course Credit, Institutional Control, and Course Type, Four-Year Institutions

Institutional Control	Course Credit					
	1	2	3	4	5	6
Lecture						
Public	2.3	2.6	2.9	3.0	3.5	3.9
Private	2.2	3.2	3.0	3.2	2.9	3.7
Lecture with lab or discussion						
Public	4.6	4.1	4.8	5.2	5.4	5.2
Private	3.3	3.6	4.1	4.6	4.6	—
Nonlecture						
Public	2.3	2.5	3.3	3.6	3.3	—
Private	3.0	3.3	3.3	3.1	—	—

Note: See Table 2.4 footnote for explanation of the dashes.

Table 2.8. Number of Courses by Course Credit, Level, and Type, Four-Year Institutions

Course Level	Course Credit					
	1	2	3	4	5	6
Lecture						
Lower undergraduate	1,453	650	9,559	2,554	278	76
Upper undergraduate	583	472	9,739	1,343	63	82
Graduate	419	314	4,468	476	—	100
Lecture with lab or discussion						
Lower undergraduate	194	316	1,415	1,319	102	15
Upper undergraduate	96	180	1,371	480	—	—
Graduate	39	38	400	97	—	—
Nonlecture						
Lower undergraduate	1,645	172	733	136	—	—
Upper undergraduate	629	368	778	142	—	—
Graduate	179	59	591	70	—	—

Note: See Table 2.4 footnote for explanation of the dashes.

Table 2.9. Mean Scheduled Time in Class per Week by Course Credit, Level, and Type, Four-Year Institutions

Course Level	Course Credit					
	1	2	3	4	5	6
Lecture						
Lower undergraduate	2.3	2.6	2.9	3.0	3.4	3.5
Upper undergraduate	2.4	2.7	2.9	3.1	3.0	4.1
Graduate	2.2	2.8	2.9	3.1	—	3.8
Lecture with lab or discussion						
Lower undergraduate	4.4	4.1	4.5	5.0	5.3	—
Upper undergraduate	4.0	4.2	4.8	5.1	—	—
Graduate	5.3	4.2	5.0	5.1	—	—
Nonlecture						
Lower undergraduate	2.2	2.8	3.7	3.6	—	—
Upper undergraduate	2.8	2.4	3.3	3.5	—	—
Graduate	2.9	2.8	3.0	2.9	—	—

Note: See Table 2.4 footnote for explanation of the dashes.

biological and life science and physical science courses are more heavily concentrated in the four-credit courses than is the case in the other disciplines, which offer most of their courses for three credits (foreign language and literature is evenly split between three- and four-credit courses). Still, regardless of the discipline and the credit value, the lecture courses with labs or discussions meet, on average, for four or five hours a week.

Table 2.10. Number of Lecture Courses by Credit and Discipline, Four-Year Institutions

	Course Credit					
Discipline	1	2	3	4	5	6
Communications	45	35	1,039	110	—	—
Education	252	201	1,971	120	—	—
Engineering	195	66	1,231	244	—	—
Foreign languages and literature	43	61	1,501	472	116	32
English language and literature	—	—	2,952	556	—	—
Biological sciences and life sciences	207	109	569	278	33	—
Mathematics	37	43	1,671	468	71	—
Physical sciences	339	64	759	301	56	—
Social sciences and history	76	—	3,938	747	—	—
Visual and performing arts	322	355	1,546	295	—	—
Health professions and related sciences	45	51	359	87	—	—
Business management and administrative services	72	125	2,497	242	—	—

Note: See Table 2.4 footnote for explanation of the dashes.

Table 2.11. Mean Scheduled Time in Class per Week by Credit and Discipline, Lecture Courses, Four-Year Institutions

	Course Credit					
Discipline	1	2	3	4	5	6
Communications	2.81	2.79	2.87	3.36	—	—
Education	2.26	2.67	2.94	3.20	—	—
Engineering	2.09	2.65	2.82	3.33	—	—
Foreign languages and literature	2.76	3.03	2.81	3.10	3.91	3.08
English language and literature	—	—	2.85	3.60	—	—
Biological sciences and life sciences	2.28	2.68	2.92	2.90	2.89	—
Mathematics	1.66	2.57	2.93	3.18	3.20	—
Physical sciences	2.62	2.95	2.94	2.65	2.68	—
Social sciences and history	2.34	—	2.90	3.03	—	—
Visual and performing arts	2.45	2.64	3.17	3.26	—	—
Health professions and related sciences	1.90	2.61	2.95	3.31	—	—
Business management and administrative services	2.54	3.20	3.02	3.41	—	—

Note: See Table 2.4 footnote for explanation of the dashes.

Course File Data Results for Two-Year Institutions

Course files were submitted by nine two-year institutions, although some of them were large multicampus districts reporting for several campuses. As with the four-year institutions' courses, each course was designated as either a lecture, lecture with a lab or discussion, or a nonlecture course. The same data-cleaning process was used for the two-year institutions as was described for the four-year institutions. An explanation of how many course records were eliminated at each stage of the data-cleaning process

Table 2.12. Number of Lecture Courses with Lab or Discussion by Credit and Discipline, Four-Year Institutions

Discipline	Course Credit					
	1	2	3	4	5	6
Communications	—	—	156	—	—	—
Education	40	—	234	—	—	—
Engineering	39	84	349	148	—	—
Foreign languages and literature	—	—	193	197	—	—
English language and literature	—	—	218	28	—	—
Biological sciences and life sciences	40	41	116	297	—	—
Mathematics	—	—	278	254	43	—
Physical sciences	—	38	111	636	38	—
Social sciences and history	—	—	453	82	—	—
Visual and performing arts	63	156	158	55	—	—
Health professions and related sciences	—	—	61	35	—	—
Business management and administrative services	—	—	203	—	—	—

Note: See Table 2.4 footnote for explanation of the dashes.

Table 2.13. Mean Scheduled Time in Class per Week by Course Credit and Discipline, Lecture Courses with Lab or Discussion, Four-Year Institutions

Discipline	Course Credit					
	1	2	3	4	5	6
Communications	—	—	4.34	—	—	—
Education	5.35	—	5.00	—	—	—
Engineering	3.22	4.29	5.02	5.50	—	—
Foreign languages and literature	—	—	4.02	5.74	—	—
English language and literature	—	—	4.25	5.13	—	—
Biological sciences and life sciences	4.35	5.40	4.88	5.72	—	—
Mathematics	—	—	4.58	4.35	5.73	—
Physical sciences	—	4.43	4.82	5.12	4.82	—
Social sciences and history	—	—	4.10	5.14	—	—
Visual and performing arts	4.39	3.86	4.48	3.76	—	—
Health professions and related sciences	—	—	3.74	4.70	—	—
Business management and administrative services	—	—	5.25	—	—	—

Note: See Table 2.4 footnote for explanation of the dashes.

is provided in the footnote of Table 2.2. This resulted in analyzable data for courses with one to five credits, but the number after data cleaning for six-credit courses was too small (only twenty-seven course records), so they were removed from the analysis.

Similar to the four-year institutions, most courses (64 percent) in the analysis files for the two-year institutions were lecture courses (4 percent were nonlecture, and 33 percent were lab or discussion). Of those lecture courses, 70 percent are offered for three credits, and 16 percent are listed as four-credit courses. As with the four-year institutions, the records do not seem to stray far from that traditional three-credit lecture. In addition, 65 percent of the lecture courses including a lab or discussion component are worth three credits, and 14 percent are offered for four credits. Perhaps surprisingly, 425 nonlectures were recorded, and 85 percent are offered for one credit.

Class or Course Hours. These data also suggest that the lecture courses at the two-year institutions have stronger relationships between course credit and amount of time in class than the four-year institutions. Although the one- and two-credit courses are still, on average, meeting for longer than may be expected based on course credit (1.99 and 2.96 hours, respectively), 41 percent of the one-credit courses meet for one hour a week, and 45 percent of the two-credit courses meet for two hours a week. The three-, four-, and five-credit classes seem to follow a strong pattern. Three-credit lecture courses meet for an average of three hours a week, four-credit lecture courses meet for an average of 3.88 hours a week, and five-credit lecture courses meet for an average of 4.89 hours a week (Table 2.14).

For lecture courses with lab or discussion components, on average, the more credits a course is worth, the longer the courses meet. However, the strength of the relationship between course credit and time in class in two-year institutions does not seem to be as strong for lecture courses with lab and discussion components as for the lecture courses alone. When comparing the two- and four-year institutions, more variation is seen in the time spent in class for these lecture-with-lab courses in the two-year institutions. In the two-year institutions studied, one-credit courses meet, on average, for 2.97 hours a week whereas the five-credit lecture with lab courses meet for an average of 5.75 hours a week. In the four-year institutions, time spent in class ranged only from 4.39 hours to 5.2 hours per week.

Table 2.14. Number of Courses and Mean Scheduled Class Time by Course Credit and Type, Two-Year Institutions

Number of Courses and Class Times	Course Credit				
	1	2	3	4	5
Lecture					
Number of courses	273	315	5,203	1,181	445
Mean scheduled class time (hr.)	1.99	2.96	3.00	3.88	4.89
Lecture with lab or discussion					
Number of courses	331	156	2,486	539	293
Mean scheduled class time (hr.)	2.97	3.33	3.97	5.07	5.75
Nonlecture					
Number of courses	359	53	—	—	—
Mean scheduled class time (hr.)	2.56	4.11	—	—	—

Note: See Table 2.4 footnote for explanation of the dashes.

As noted above, most nonlecture courses in two-year institutions are offered for one credit. Beyond this point, it is difficult to draw any conclusions about the nonlecture courses simply because there were enough records for reporting in only one- and two-credit courses.

Patterns by Course Discipline. As was the case for four-year institutions, no strong disciplinary pattern was shown among the two-year respondents; regardless of the discipline, three-credit courses seem to be the most prevalent. For pure lecture courses, a small amount of variation was seen with respect to discipline (Table 2.15). Most of the foreign languages and literature courses were listed as four-credit classes. In addition, computer and information sciences and mathematics were relatively evenly distributed as three and four credits. In time spent in class for the lecture courses, the clearest finding (shown in Table 2.16) is that three-credit courses meet for about three hours a week, regardless of the discipline. The only exception is the three-credit computer and information sciences courses, which met, on average, for 3.93 hours a week.

Again, most of the lecture courses with lab or discussion components, regardless of discipline, are still worth three credits (Table 2.17). Interestingly, computer and information sciences is an exception for the lecture-with-lab courses, in addition to being an exception for the pure lecture courses. A large number of lecture-with-lab courses in this discipline are offered for one credit. In addition, the physical sciences courses are distributed across three, four, and five credits, as opposed to being heavily concentrated in one credit worth.

The patterns are not as straightforward when examining the time spent in class for the lecture-with-lab courses (Table 2.18). Overall, these courses appear to meet for a longer time than might be expected based on their credit worth. This is especially true for the courses in the physical sciences,

Table 2.15. Number of Lecture Courses by Course Credit and Discipline, Two-Year Institutions

	Course Credit				
Discipline	1	2	3	4	5
Communications	—	—	62	—	—
Computer and information sciences	—	—	138	176	—
Education	—	—	262	—	—
Foreign languages and literature	—	—	31	124	—
English language and literature	—	—	1,551	73	147
Mathematics	—	—	424	333	56
Physical sciences	—	—	65	—	—
Social sciences and history	—	—	625	—	39
Visual and performing arts	76	50	298	—	—
Health professions and related sciences	—	54	108	—	—
Business management and administrative services	—	36	560	281	50

Note: See Table 2.4 footnote for explanation of the dashes.

Table 2.16. Mean Scheduled Time in Class per Week by Course Credit and Discipline, Lecture Courses, Two-Year Institutions

Discipline	Course Credit				
	1	2	3	4	5
Communications	—	—	2.98	—	—
Computer and information sciences	—	—	3.93	3.76	—
Education	—	2.20	2.94	—	—
Foreign languages and literature	—	—	2.95	4.07	—
English language and literature	—	—	2.96	4.00	5.03
Mathematics	—	—	3.01	3.81	4.71
Physical sciences	—	—	2.98	—	—
Social sciences and history	—	—	2.95	—	5.00
Visual and performing arts	2.36	3.06	2.96	—	—
Health professions and related sciences	—	2.26	2.99	—	—
Business management and administrative services	—	2.64	2.92	3.62	4.81

Note: See Table 2.4 footnote for explanation of the dashes.

visual and performing arts, and the health professions and related sciences. For example, three- and four-credit courses in the physical sciences discipline meet for an average of about five hours a week whereas the five-credit courses meet for an average of well over six hours a week (6.56 hours). This is not too surprising because a good amount of labs, practicums, and studio work is probably more likely to occur in the arts, health-related sciences, and the physical sciences, which anecdotally meet for longer periods than the typical discussion sections.

A breakdown in courses by discipline was not completed for the non-lecture courses because the sample size was too small in the two-year institution files.

Table 2.17. Number of Lecture Courses with Labs by Course Credit and Discipline, Two-Year Institutions

Discipline	Course Credit				
	1	2	3	4	5
Computer and information sciences	158	—	53	77	—
Education	58	—	—	—	—
Foreign languages and literature	—	—	—	—	—
English language and literature	31	—	699	—	37
Mathematics	—	—	206	—	—
Physical sciences	—	—	158	82	103
Social sciences and history	—	—	140	—	—
Visual and performing arts	31	—	331	70	—
Health professions and related sciences	—	33	—	—	—
Business management and administrative services	33	—	330	—	—

Note: See Table 2.4 footnote for explanation of the dashes.

Table 2.18. Mean Scheduled Time in Class per Week by Course Credit and Discipline, Lecture Courses with Labs, Two-Year Institutions

Discipline	Course Credit				
	1	2	3	4	5
Computer and information sciences	3.17	—	3.21	3.12	—
Education	2.95	—	—	—	—
Foreign languages and literature	—	—	—	—	—
English language and literature	2.81	—	3.97	—	5.14
Mathematics	—	—	3.16	—	—
Physical sciences	—	—	5.14	5.18	6.56
Social sciences and history	—	—	2.88	—	—
Visual and performing arts	2.00	—	5.09	5.68	—
Health professions and related sciences	—	4.49	—	—	—
Business management and administrative services	2.94	—	3.16	—	—

Note: See Table 2.4 footnote for explanation of the dashes.

Findings and Conclusions

The survey results are clearly incomplete and somewhat confusing. Perhaps if the questions had been asked differently, the data would make more sense. As it is, the results tell us relatively little about the ways that credits are assigned to time in class. Nuances about the nature of instruction and the differences between different types of instruction are masked by the ways that course work gets translated into registrars' record files. These results certainly cannot be used to reach general conclusions about the extent of instructional innovation in higher education. Some general truths seem to emerge from the data, however, which are telling in themselves. In this study's sample,

The predominant mode of recording learning is through the use of the credit-hour measure. This is true for both four- and two-year institutions and in public and private institutions.

Most four-year institutions do not have internal policies that define what credit hours are, either for students or for faculty. So although the measure is required, it is not defined. This surely means that institutions deliberately allow for much variation in how the measures are awarded and are not particularly concerned about consistency in procedures for assigning credits to learning.

Two-year institutions were more likely than four-year institutions to have written policies for determining the number of credits a new course is worth.

Lecture courses are the predominant mode of instruction. This is true regardless of type or control of institution, level of the course, or the academic discipline the course falls under. We do not know, however, the extent to which different types of instructional delivery (team teaching, Internet-supplemented classroom work, or service learning) are getting reported as "lectures" simply because there are no unique codes for these different types of instructional delivery.

Courses are most commonly offered for three credits. Although there are some exceptions to this—for example, the baccalaureate institutions studied offer four-credit courses more often—three-credit courses are still the overall trend.

At the four-year institutions, credit does not seem to be awarded based on time spent in class, even when looking at the lecture courses. In contrast, at the two-year institutions, the lecture courses seemed to have a strong relationship between credit awarded and time spent in class. However, the relationship does not appear as strong for lecture courses with lab and discussion components.

Overall, time in class seems to vary less than the credit awarded. This suggests that institutional habits about use of time are less flexible than for recording student learning. Although this is most true for the four-year institutions, it is also generally the case in two-year institutions. In four-year institutions, the lectures seemed to hover around three hours per week, regardless of credit worth and lectures with labs or discussions around four or five hours, regardless of the credit for which the course is offered.

We expected to find distinctive patterns by type and control of institution, discipline of the course, and level of instruction for four-year institutions, reflecting variable or inconsistent criteria for awarding credit. For the most part, we did not. Baccalaureate institutions offered most of their lecture courses for four credits, whereas the other types of institutions offered most of their courses for three credits. In the public institutions, the lecture courses are highly concentrated in three-credit courses whereas lecture courses at the private institutions are almost evenly concentrated in three- and four-credit courses. Slightly more variation in credit awarded was found at the private institutions. Overall, strong patterns by discipline were not apparent. Lecture courses with lab or discussion components in the biological and life sciences and physical sciences are more heavily concentrated in the four-credit courses than in the other disciplines, which offer most of these courses for three credits (foreign languages and literature is evenly split between three- and four-credit courses). Still, regardless of the discipline and the credit worth, the lecture courses with labs or discussions meet, on average, for four or five hours a week. There were also no distinct patterns by course level.

A different picture emerges for the two-year colleges. We expected to see little variation in the awarding of credits in two-year institutions, and in this case the data supported our hypothesis. Two-year institutions had less variation, at least for lecture courses, than did the four-year institutions. They also reported having internal policies and external guidelines for assigning credits to classes much more frequently than is the case for the four-year institutions. Although all of these findings are tentative, they suggest that the community colleges are more heavily regulated in these matters than are the four-year institutions.

We remain skeptical about the essential validity of the data for all sectors, however, and are not convinced that what is recorded in the course file accurately reflects practices within institutions. Is what is recorded in the course file indicative of what is truly going on with respect to instruction? Or is it possible that many innovative teaching practices are being employed and are being "translated" for reporting and recording purposes into a typical three-credit lecture? It is important to reemphasize here that many reported courses could not be included in the analysis because course credit or time was not included in the file. These could be more innovative courses that we were not able to capture here. In addition, the data presented here indicate how course work is recorded, not necessarily how material is being taught. It is possible that some "outside-of-the-box" teaching methods are being recorded to look like traditional courses simply to fit into the traditional recording structures. Nonetheless, if the data are "true," they strongly indicate that the modality of the three-hour, three-days-a-week lecture class still essentially defines how teaching is delivered in institutions of higher education. The kinds of variations in patterns that would be expected because of the different disciplines, faculty, and curricula seem not to exist. Although the metric of the student credit hour cannot be said to be entirely responsible for this state of sameness, it may well be contributing to it.

Reference

National Center for Education Statistics. *Classification of Instructional Programs—2002*. Washington, D.C.: National Center for Education Statistics, U.S. Department of Education, 2002.

JESSICA M. SHEDD is a research analyst in the Office of Institutional Research and Planning at the University of Maryland, College Park.

3

The premise of the credit hour is the equation of student learning with class time. Leaders at institutions particularly known for innovations in student learning have found ways to work with and around the metric, although it remains an obstacle to innovation at most institutions.

The Credit Hour as a Potential Barrier to Innovation: Lessons from Innovative Institutions

Thomas Ehrlich

This chapter reports on the results of interviews with individuals involved in different institutions known for instructional innovation to learn their experiences in leading institutional change and their perceptions about the extent to which the metrics of the credit hour either helped or impeded their efforts. Using advice provided by the Project Advisory Committee (see the appendix in Editors' Notes), we selected eleven institutions believed to be national leaders in instructional innovation. The institutions chosen represent a range of innovative approaches, including delivery of instruction, pedagogy, curriculum, and emphasis on learning outcomes. Telephone interviews were conducted with officials from these institutions to learn the extent to which the metric of the credit hour, as used to measure student learning or work, has been an obstacle to their change efforts. Each was asked questions designed to elicit how the institution had grappled with issues involving credit hours both internally and externally. Documents were sent to each institution listed below. (Specific comments were received from Alverno College, University of Phoenix, New College of Florida, and Excelsior College.)

Innovative Institutions

Alverno College in Milwaukee is a small nonprofit private Catholic college for women founded in the nineteenth century. Since the 1970s, it has been a national leader in the movement to establish the outcomes of an undergraduate education. Alverno College has established eight "abilities" and six levels at which mastery is to be demonstrated.

California State University (CSU) at Monterey Bay is a small residential campus of the California state university (public comprehensive universities) system. Sited on a former military base, CSU at Monterey Bay was founded both to promote outcomes-based education and to encourage innovation on other CSU campuses. Community-service learning is widespread throughout the curriculum.

Charter Oak State College in New Britain, Connecticut, a public college, was founded by the Connecticut legislature in 1973 to enable state students to learn through distance-based education. All of its courses are provided via the Internet.

Empire State College in Saratoga Springs, New York, was established in 1971 as part of the State University of New York (SUNY) system. It has the particular mission of developing and using new modes of individualized instruction with a strong emphasis on distance education. It offers courses through a variety of delivery models.

Excelsior College (formerly Regents College) in Albany, New York, is a private nonprofit institution founded thirty years ago to serve working adults. It publicizes that students can gain Excelsior College credit for past learning and take courses in any field that are offered at any accredited college or university through distance-based education and working with Excelsior faculty.

Evergreen State College in Olympia, Washington, a residential, public campus, was founded in 1967 and has its own board of trustees. All of its programs are interdisciplinary, and classes are run on a block system. Students enroll in a single program, one per semester. Evergreen has gained a national reputation for leadership in developing models of collaborative learning.

New College of Florida in Sarasota was initially founded in 1960 as a private nonprofit college but became a part of the University of South Florida (a campus of the public state system) in 1975. A 2001 change in governance in higher education in Florida has changed it once again into an independent public honors college. Students negotiate an academic contract with faculty covering their expected work. They are not assigned credit for courses but rather work toward fulfilling their contracts.

Thomas Edison State College in Trenton, New Jersey, founded three decades ago, was created by the state to promote distance-based education. This public college offers opportunities for students to document the college-level knowledge they already have and to take courses via the Internet.

Tusculum College in Greeneville, Tennessee, a small, private, liberal arts college, shapes a common curriculum around nine outcomes or competencies. Blocks of courses have been organized into a core curriculum.

University of Phoenix, a private for-profit institution, has become one of the largest providers of higher education in the country, serving more than 100,000 students, including about 30,000 via the Internet. Students are all working adults, and faculty teams design courses that are then taught with common assessments.

Western Governors University (WGU) in Salt Lake City was founded to provide a new approach to articulating the outcomes of undergraduate education and to offer a performance-based means for students to achieve those outcomes through distance-based education. It is supported by a consortium of governors from Western states, excluding California.

Surprisingly, we learned that these institutions, with the exception of WGU, did not find credit hours a significant impediment to doing what they set out to do in the realm of student learning. They all found ways to equate the learning of their students to credit hours, at least to the extent necessary to overcome or circumvent the barriers that credit hours might otherwise have imposed. Although external requirements that learning be recorded in credit hours were at least an irritant, all of the institutions except WGU found ways to work around the problem.

Why? On reflection, we concluded that those involved in leading these innovative colleges and universities had a clear idea of what they wanted to do in the realm of student learning and how they wanted to do it. They developed visions of the learning modes they sought to encourage—visions that had relative institutional cohesion and coherence. This is true of institutions that sought to serve new or expanding markets for distance-based education through the Internet. They are successfully serving mobile student populations that may want particular courses but not an entire undergraduate education. It is also true of institutions that framed their vision of student learning as an integrative approach to the knowledge and skills to be gained from an undergraduate education, with an emphasis either on the outcomes of that education, as at Alverno College, CSU at Monterey Bay, and Tusculum College, or on the educational process, as at Evergreen College. WGU has sought to be in both camps and to create its own market in the process. This effort to meet two innovative objectives simultaneously may have contributed to the difficulties that institution has faced. Its problems, as discussed below, relate more to issues of market than to concerns about credit hours for external purposes, but those concerns have had an effect. The other institutions faced numerous and troublesome hurdles in developing their programs, and some still face major problems, but they were able to deal with the need of external groups to define the learning of their students in credit hours.

If this conclusion about innovative institutions is accurate, we nonetheless doubt that it tells much about the potential of the credit hour as a substantial constrictor of innovation. At colleges and universities that have not adopted institution-wide innovative approaches to teaching and learning and where so often the only thing holding the institution together is the accounting system, we suspect that the credit hour is a major barrier to innovation because, of course, it is built into the accounting system. It is the coin of the realm for academic and administrative measurement in higher education, with its uses spanning beyond measuring teaching and learning to a host of administrative, financial, and regulatory requirements. In public institutions, particularly, the credit hour is embedded in regulations about courses, residency requirements, academic calendars, and budgeting systems that collectively become huge obstacles to overcome. (These issues are explored in subsequent chapters.)

Distance-Education Providers

Institutions that define themselves as distance-learning providers and that serve mobile and primarily part-time student populations through distance-mediated course delivery face an obvious problem. Credit hours have come to be viewed at least in part as a measure of time spent in a classroom, and students at institutions such as Charter Oak State College, for example, do not spend any time in a classroom. Rather, they are awarded credit for work done on-line, as reviewed by Charter Oak's faculty. (Thomas Edison College and Excelsior College follow similar approaches.) In terms of past work, students are awarded credit for their proficiency in a field through either a standard proficiency test or a narrative portfolio that gives evidence that what they have learned is the equivalent of a course in the catalogue of an accredited campus somewhere in the country. All of these institutions avoid problems by translating their credits into credit hours when called on to do so by outside agencies or by other institutions to which their students want to transfer. Charter Oak State College, for example, uses credit-hour language in the sense that students gain credit for courses, generally three or four credits per course, and that credit is translated in credit hours. This seems sufficient to satisfy most other colleges and universities to which students want to transfer, as well as federal and state officials.

At Excelsior College, Academic Vice President Paula Peinovich reports that in developing a course, the faculty involved, many of whom may hold appointments at other institutions as well, start with the outcomes that should result from the course. They have in mind the outcomes of a three-credit-hour course from their prior teaching. They then work backwards to design the course so that those outcomes are achieved by students taking the course. In the process of developing a course, therefore, they do not try to reconcile the reality that some three-credit-hour courses require much more work than others, both by students and by the faculty member in charge, even within the same institution. But faculty try to hold to a common norm among the Excelsior College courses so that the amount of student work required to meet the prescribed outcomes of a three-credit-hour course is roughly similar across disciplines, based on the judgment of the faculty. The credit-hour hurdle is avoided by adopting this approach and by a willingness to translate Excelsior College outcomes into the credit-hour metric.

Like CSU at Monterey Bay within the CSU system, Empire State College was started within the SUNY system to encourage and facilitate experimentation with new approaches to undergraduate education that might benefit the whole system. It was designed in part to help stave off pressure to build more SUNY campuses in low-enrollment areas and to promote collaboration among SUNY campuses in serving state students. The Empire State College faculty also adopted a system that avoided the credit-hour problem. The system was based on a New York State policy that equated nonclassroom study to credit hours, a policy that had been in place for some time. The policy, in essence, equated forty to forty-five hours of "study" to three credit hours for purposes such as independent study, internships, and distance instruction. Following this policy, the Empire State College faculty said that a semester credit hour should equal forty hours of work per semester, wherever that work was done—in class or out of class. The faculty try to ensure that they assign a total of 120 hours of work—for the average student—for a three-credit-hour course. Apparently both state and federal officials accepted the approach.

A major problem that these distance-based education institutions have faced concerns federal student financial aid, having to do with academic calendars, minimum number of weeks of instruction, definitions of full- and part-time, and restrictions on distance learning. These requirements originated in federal efforts to address financial aid fraud that in the 1970s and 1980s was perpetrated by institutions that bilked students for tuition (and student loan) resources but did not offer bona fide instructional programs. Some operated as "correspondence schools," which federal law treats identically to distance-based education (these issues are discussed at length in Chapter Six). The growing absurdity of the federal requirements, however, gave rise to a student aid demonstration program designed to test alternatives to conventional, time-based regulations. WGU, Charter Oak State College, and other institutions have applied for and received demonstration program status, making it easier for them to provide student aid to their students.

Curriculum Innovators

Another set of institutions are innovators in undergraduate teaching and learning. Unlike the distance-based education providers discussed above, these institutions serve primarily full-time undergraduate student populations seeking a baccalaureate degree (although a significant share of Alverno College students attend its Weekend College). Students transferring in and out of these institutions are not as large a problem as they are for the distance-based education providers, and as a result these institutions are better able to approach comprehensive curriculum development. Although challenging or changing the credit hour itself was not consciously perceived by the leaders of these institutions as the goal of their instructional reform, all were motivated by some degree of disenchantment with the conventional approach to defining an undergraduate education as an accumulation of course credits totaling 120 units (or, on some campuses, thirty-two courses).

Among these other innovators, the most common approach is simply to translate whatever the institution is doing into credit hours, much like those focusing on distance education. At Evergreen State College, for example, students register for one program per year, and each is given forty-eight quarter-hour credits. A full load (and 90 percent of students are full-time) is sixteen quarter units or four courses of four hours each. But there are not really separate courses, just programs. A freshman, for example, may be in the "Great Books" program for her first year, and that will be her entire effort for the year. The former provost at Evergreen State College, Barbara Smith, thinks that the fifty-minute hour is a more serious impediment to good teaching and learning than credit hours, and Evergreen has none. The standard block of time is a three-hour period, which includes both plenary sessions and workshops. The whole approach at Evergreen is to avoid "atomizing" students and to build student capacities to learn collaboratively as part of a team.

The founders of Evergreen State College had a vision of an undergraduate educational experience designed to foster collaborative learning, and every program is based on that vision. Realizing the vision has taken an enormous amount of time, energy, and effort, and within that setting, overcoming the constraints of the credit-hour metric seems relatively minor.

A similar story can be told based on the experience of CSU at Monterey Bay. The campus was added as the twenty-first in the CSU system in 1994, in part because a former military base—on a prime piece of coastal property—became available. But even more important, the chancellor and other senior administrators of the system saw an opportunity to bring innovation to the whole system through the leadership of a new campus founded on an integrated concept of the learning required for an undergraduate education. Like Empire State College, the campus from the start had the support of the state educational bureaucracy and the system leadership, and both helped to overcome barriers to innovation by the campus within the system. One key feature was the development of thirteen "university learning requirements" such as "community participation," "creative and artistic expression," and "democratic participation." Graduates must demonstrate proficiency in each university learning requirement. Several other innovative requirements, including service-learning courses and a senior capstone experience, were also adopted. From the outset, a "vision statement" has served to guide campus decisions. The document is posted throughout the campus, and new faculty and staff sign a copy in a public ceremony at the beginning of each year. The campus has been marked by conflicts almost from the outset, but it has had little trouble translating student work into credit hours for internal CSU purposes, for other state and federal purposes, and for purposes of student transfers.

Both Alverno and Tusculum colleges also have shaped their curricula in terms of explicit outcomes, although in somewhat different ways. Alverno was and remains a national leader in this realm and has published extensively about making an undergraduate education a coherent experience that involves "learning that lasts," in the felicitous phrase that is the title of a recent book about Alverno's curricular efforts (Mentkowski and others, 1999). Tusculum has focused particularly on educating better citizens, although its competency program is similar in many ways to that of Alverno.

New College of Florida emphasizes that its students take courses and are not assigned credits or grades. Rather, they have a "contract" for each semester, signed by a student and faculty advisor, that specifies courses and other academic activities for that semester. Students must complete seven contracts to graduate. All students must register for full-time status, and that means paying for sixteen hours of course work per semester under the Florida public university billing system. That payment enables them to develop an academic contract with a faculty member that may include any number of courses, internships, volunteer work, and independent study or any combination of these or other academic activities agreed on by the student and the faculty member. Each signed contract is considered the equivalent of sixteen credit hours for both internal and external purposes in the first semester and twenty credit hours in the second semester. (January is an independent study period, which is counted as part of the second semester.) If students transfer, New College recommends that their courses are the equivalent of four credit hours each. State and federal authorities accept this approach. As at Alverno and Tusculum, therefore, New College was also shaped by a vision of education, and in that context credit hours were minor hurdles.

The major exception is WGU, and it deserves special mention, along with Phoenix University, for a somewhat different reason. WGU was founded, according to its vice president and chief academic officer, Chip Johnstone, in part because of frustration with both the quality and the measures of quality of outcomes, symbolized by the credit hour. Those involved believed that the credit hour alone was not a sound measure of competency. It was not, in their view, even a measure of effort but solely a measure of seat time. WGU does not award credit hours or other credits. The only way to succeed is to prove competency through an assessment. WGU now has two bachelor's degrees, a Bachelor of Science in business, with an emphasis on information technology management, and a Bachelor of Science in computer information systems.

More generally, WGU is focusing on three primary areas, business, information technology, and teacher education. Its market is older working adults, not eighteen- to twenty-four-year-old students. Each of the three areas is guided by a council of a six- to nine-member mix of higher education and practicing professional experts. They determine the degree structure and competencies. Then a national assessment council establishes the assessments that will be used. Each enrolled student has a mentor (they are located all over the country and are the "faculty"). Mentors help students decide what they need to learn to prepare for the assessments. WGU offers twelve hundred courses from forty different providers in its network. The mentor is a bridge between resources and students. Courses are seen as just avenues to competencies. Theoretically, WGU does not care about anything else.

A key break for WGU was the agreement by federal officials supervising Title IV, Financial Aid, to use WGU as one of its demonstration projects in terms both of part-time or full-time and satisfactory academic progress. Otherwise, the federal restrictions on distance learning and academic calendars would have precluded WGU students from gaining access to financial aid.

WGU has made compromises to allow a better translation of the WGU competency credentials into credit-hour measures that students can use in the workplace and in other institutions. Toward this end, the university has negotiated articulation agreements with both two- and four-year institutions to smooth student flow in and out of WGU. With the two-year institutions, it has negotiated articulation agreements with a number of community colleges to reward students who have successfully completed the transfer curriculum with upper-division WGU status, the equivalent of 60 units of 120 needed for a WGU degree. Similar agreements have been developed with some four-year campuses so that lower-division WGU competencies are accepted as the equivalent of sixty units of credit at those campuses. WGU also prepares transcripts that translate the WGU competency requirements into conventional blocks of credit units to assist students who want to transfer to other campuses. For example, the WGU degree is translated into 120 semester credits. If 20 percent of the competency requirements are in language and communication, then these are translated into twenty-four transcript credits. WGU administrators felt that they had to accommodate the credit-hour translation because registrars at other institutions would not recognize WGU's competency measures if they were not framed in credit-hour terms.

Obtaining regional accreditation was also a struggle for WGU. The university could have easily applied for accreditation from one or more of the national accrediting agencies, such as the Distance Education Training Council, that are accustomed to working with distance-learning institutions operating in many states. Because the goal of the institution was to stimulate comprehensive higher educational reform, however, the decision was made to seek regional accreditation, widely considered to be the most prestigious form of higher education accreditation. WGU operates in several regions, so this decision meant that the university was effectively challenging the organization of regional accreditation, along with the quality criteria used for review. As a result, several of the regional accreditors formed a special consortium for the sole purpose of working with WGU.

A working group of accrediting commission staff drawn from the four regions making up WGU was formed to work with the university's staff. Much time was spent at the outset of the process in deliberating whether WGU qualified as an "institution of higher education" for purposes of regional accreditation and whether as a result its application for accreditation review could even be accepted. This basic issue of accreditability took some time to resolve, but ultimately the group decided in favor of recognizing the institution, despite its unconventional structure. The application for candidacy for regional accreditation was accepted, although final accreditation was still pending as this chapter was being written.

In the meanwhile, WGU has moved forward to secure full accreditation from the Distance Education and Training Council. Because this council is the body that accredits many of the military education programs, this accreditation is a big plus for WGU.

By the summer of 2001, however, WGU had only 1,150 students taking at least one course, with 250 of those seeking a degree. Despite all the hyperbole that WGU would be flooded with students, this has not happened. Why not? The problem is that students can choose from among a range of distance providers. They overwhelmingly now are taking courses at campuses and just want a few more via the Internet. They need easy transfer of credit, and that means credit hours. They do not want to have to explain to another institution all about competencies and assessments. So they do not choose WGU. It will take a long time to change this.

For the future, Johnstone sees a big potential market in articulation agreements with state governments (about six of these already exist) and companies (Novell is the only one currently) to use the state or company Web site for employees to enable access to WGU courses. So, for example, the National Urban League requires its employees to prove competency X and Y to be promoted to job Z. WGU staff translates those competencies into course work and enables the employees to prove the competencies through its system. Some states also require their employees to prove competencies for various purposes, and WGU can be the means. Does this mean that the whole WGU system will shift its goal from a primary focus on degrees, which it had at the outset, to a focus simply on courses that have credit hours attached to them? Probably it will not, although Johnstone expects that degree programs will not be the only thing driving the future development of the WGU. He expects that many students will come to WGU, as some come already, to master competencies that lead to a certificate or a job qualification, rather than to a degree. To do that, they will often (though not always) take courses that have credit hours attached. The WGU transcript will list those credit hours attached to courses taken through its providers, but it will also clearly indicate the specific competencies achieved.

In short, for WGU, the credit-hour metric caused big hurdles in the areas of federal financial aid, accreditation, and transfer, but those hurdles have been mostly overcome. The biggest hurdle is student acceptance of competencies, and that has not been overcome. For many students, the marketplace offers too many other options to risk investing their time and money in an unproven experiment. At the same time, WGU is still determined to prove itself through defining what is needed to reform undergraduate education, and the institution seeks to use political leverage to force markets to work to its advantage.

The University of Phoenix is now the largest private institution of higher education in the country (by far larger than the largest private nonprofit university) and the fastest growing institution of higher education in the country. All of its students are working adults; having a job is a requirement for admission. Of its more than 100,000 students, 75,000 attend class and 25,000 are on-line (it is also the largest on-line institution). The average age is thirty-five years, and average work experience is twelve years. The university has a core of full-time faculty on each campus, plus many practitioners who are like adjunct faculty and are part-time.

In light of its student population, the University of Phoenix designed its curriculum model so that in-class students attend class for four hours once per week for five or six weeks (undergraduates attend for five weeks, graduates for six). Students who miss more than one of the four or six weekly sessions are required to take the entire course over again. They are in classes of fourteen students per class. Each class is divided into a learning group of three to five students. Each learning group meets several hours each week. So students are engaged twenty-four hours with an instructor per course and an additional twenty hours with a learning group. The university emphasizes students as learners with faculty as coaches, and student learning is measured by assessment examinations accompanied by assessments before and after the examinations.

Like the other providers, the University of Phoenix is forced to translate its courses into credit hours, and the typical five-week course is considered the equivalent of three credit hours. Most states seem to accept this approach. Some, such as New York and New Jersey, however, have given the university a hard time, not simply because of the credit-hour issue, but also because of claims of inadequate faculty contact. This charge has led to a change in procedure that now requires that learning-group sessions physically meet with a faculty person once a week. The university did not resist this requirement because its leaders believe that time on task is important, much as they did not like it being imposed on them. They view their attendance requirements as superior to those of most institutions that do not require students to attend any classes. Their contention is that most institutions measure schedules, rather than time on learning. Most colleges accept University of Phoenix credits without a problem because it is regionally accredited by the North Central Commission on Learning. Some institutions do resist the measures of credit hours, and so the learning process continues through constant dialogue. The view of officials at the University of Phoenix is that much of the resistance to the university stems from fear of competition, rather than concern about quality.

The University of Phoenix has ongoing struggles with federal financial aid officials, who resisted approval because the university allegedly did not meet the twelve-hour rule, but now it is a pilot demonstration site. Despite this, the independent inspector general raised concerns about the unconventional academic calendars and failure to demonstrate "academic progress" and demanded $60 million in back payments from the institution. The university finally settled for a payment of $6 million, but it is required to provide a huge paper trail to show that it meets attendance and academic progress rules.

Ironically, the on-line University of Phoenix courses have met with fewer regulatory hurdles. The university uses a similar format to that of its on-site courses. Cohorts of students (the average is nine) take a course. They must sign on five times per week. They download materials, do assignments, and so forth. Scores on outcomes assessments are actually slightly higher for on-line students than for those taking courses in class, but that may reflect a selection bias because pretest scores are also slightly higher. States like New York and New Jersey have no problems because the courses are seen as coming from Arizona and thus not subject to state regulations. Federal officials have not raised problems, either.

Conclusions

All of the innovative institutions, except WGU, largely solved their problems with credit hours by converting everything they were doing into course-equivalent blocks and then, when necessary, assigning credit hours to those blocks. WGU, by contrast, does not base its program on courses, and it has had problems with credit hours from its founding. In this sense, it could be said that the difference is less in the innovation of delivery or credentialing than in the organization of the curriculum in course-equivalent terms. Excelsior State College is examination based, for example, but was able to dodge the credit-hour problem because the unit for what the institution does in teaching and learning is the "course," and courses are designated with number of credit hours when needed for such purposes as student transfers and graduate schools. Although Excelsior and the others are academic innovators, they are not pushing the edge of the "academic accounting" dimension of the credit-hour paradigm. The course-based requirement could nonetheless be an impediment to academic innovation for institutions that serve highly mobile student markets and try to move into educational modules that do not translate back into courses.

The institutions discussed here that are experimenting with the most comprehensive types of curricular and learning reforms are probably able to do so because they are working with stable student cohorts of primarily full-time, traditional undergraduates. We also suspect that these kinds of innovations present even more serious barriers to measures of faculty workload. Those issues are treated separately in Chapter Four. At this point, it is enough to point to the problem of a faculty member or team of faculty members who may be assigned to coach on-line many hundreds or even thousands of students enrolled in many courses offered simultaneously. The students may earn, for example, three credit hours per course, but allocation of faculty workload and the translation of that workload into credit hours for accounting purposes could be more of a challenge.

As we have seen, except for the case at WGU, the problems of credit hours have been minimized by nimble college and university officials who found ways to translate what their institutions were doing into credit hours when necessary. It is still clear that most of them had to modify plans designed solely to promote good teaching and learning, but these accommodations do not seem fundamental. WGU continues to face a competitive problem because its offering—competencies—is often not viewed by students (and those advising them) as currency, most often measured in credit hours, in the marketplace.

Despite that other innovative institutions were able to work around the problems of the credit hour, this review suggests that the metric itself, as well as the external enforcement of it, can be a major obstacle to instructional innovation in higher education. The credit hour has the advantage of being a highly flexible measure that can be defined by the provider in terms that have some meaning within the institution. It is also a measure that has "street value" as a commonly understood indicator of learning and activity. (One of its strengths for administrators, of course, is that pressure is rarely applied to go "behind" the credit hour to ask either how much learning or how much activity it reflects.) Institutions, students, governments, employers, accreditors, and other countries recognize the credit hour as a measure of learning, even if the learning has not occurred or the standards of learning are too low. But this flexibility means that even when the credit hour itself is not a barrier to instructional innovation or innovation in the mode of delivering learning, its use results in allowing—even encouraging—institutions that are not interested in the curricular integrity of a baccalaureate degree or in instructional effectiveness to avoid addressing issues of student performance of learning objectives. And because the credit hour has such public currency as a metric, it does not have to be contextualized as part of a larger effort to articulate the aims of an undergraduate curriculum or of how those aims are to be realized. The credit hour contributes, therefore, to the atomization of student learning through the avoidance of developing better measures of learning outcomes.

Reference

Mentkowski, M., and others. *Learning That Lasts: Integrating Learning, Development, and Performance in College and Beyond.* San Francisco: Jossey-Bass, 1999.

THOMAS EHRLICH is a senior scholar at the Carnegie Foundation for the Advancement of Teaching.

*The credit hour is the common metric for measuring
faculty instructional workload and is a part of a larger
system that makes innovation more difficult.*

The Credit Hour and Faculty Instructional Workload

Thomas Ehrlich

This chapter focuses on the role of the credit hour as a measure of faculty workload. Research was conducted through interviews with academic administrators in public and private institutions, accompanied by a review of faculty workload policies available mainly through the Internet. The primary focus of the analysis has been to learn the extent to which the metric of the credit hour, as embedded in faculty workload policies, is a barrier to institutional innovation. We have been particularly interested in finding evidence of innovations in faculty workload policies that recognize alternative calibrations to the credit hour to accommodate distance-based learning, outcomes-based instruction, and other measures of faculty activity such as service and research.

The chapter begins with a general discussion of the metric of the credit hour and faculty workload policies. It then turns to a review of the issue in private institutions, followed by a review of policies in public institutions. The chapter concludes with some examples of institutional experiments with alternatives to the credit hour as a measure of faculty work.

General Overview of the Credit Hour and Faculty Workload

The story of how the credit hour evolved, outlined by Jessica Shedd in Chapter One, shows that it took hold early on in terms of measuring faculty workload along with student learning. Many if not most institutions start, implicitly if not explicitly, with the three-credit lecture course as the

NEW DIRECTIONS FOR HIGHER EDUCATION, no. 122, Summer 2003 © Wiley Periodicals, Inc.

generally accepted measure of class load. A course that met for three fifty-minute hours became a three-credit-hour course for purposes of faculty workload, just as it was for purposes of student learning. Faculty were expected to teach for a given number of credit hours per year, semester, or quarter. In the context of faculty workload, the credit hour frequently refers to student-faculty classroom contact hours, rather than to credits. But the measure is still of credit hours.

The credit-hour system of measuring faculty course-contact hours worked well enough when lectures and the fifty-minute hour predominated, and the exceptions were sufficiently circumscribed, so that ad hoc translations in credit hours were readily possible for other pedagogies on the one hand and other class lengths on the other. A science course that met three hours a week, for example, might involve a faculty member in supervising an additional hour or two of lab work, and the faculty member would be credited with four or five credit hours instead of just three. As instruction became more variegated in all dimensions, however, the application of the metric often became more arbitrary.

As this review shows, the factors that have an effect on the assignment of credits in faculty workload are rarely matters of institutional planning and design. Institutions such as Alverno College in Milwaukee are the exceptions (see Chapter Three). But at most colleges and universities, even public ones, there are no clear guidelines, and individual faculty judgments and departmental practices and customs all play a role. To the extent that flexibility exists on a campus, innovation may be allowed though not encouraged. When union agreements are involved, instructional arrangements become more regularized; innovations in instruction may be even more difficult.

Part of the reason for the seeming arbitrariness is that instruction is not all that faculty members are expected to do. The classroom contact hour, translated through credit hours, may be a clumsy measure of teaching time, but it nevertheless has some face validity as a measure of instructional workload. Research and service are the two other main categories of responsibilities at all except community colleges, which do not generally expect their faculty to engage in research. Most institutions do not try to translate either the research or the service of their faculty into credit hours, nor do they generally use some other metric to measure effort in these realms. Rather, most have reporting requirements and periodic reviews of research and service for purposes of faculty compensation, promotion, and tenure. These policies probably have deeper influences on instructional delivery and innovation than counting the credit hours.

The metric of the classroom contact hour, translated into the credit hour, is likely to have a deeper influence on part-time and adjunct faculty than on full-time tenured and tenure-track faculty. This is because they are explicitly paid on the basis of classes taught and not for a larger body of professional work. Because the number of part-time faculty has grown, this could mean that the metric of classroom contact and credit hours is becoming a more rather than a less influential lever of institutional policy. This category teaches a majority of classes in community colleges and in many comprehensive universities, other campuses, and distance-learning institutions. At research universities, teaching assistants who are also graduate students provide much of the instruction. At most institutions, all of these instructors are paid on the basis of courses taught, and courses are usually measured by contact hours in the classroom. As a result, they have no financial incentive to change their approach to teaching, particularly if change risks a loss in credit and contact hours. Many instructors are under great pressures as a result of teaching at two or three different campuses on a part-time basis. This mode of compensation on a per-course basis, in fact, probably stifles innovation more than any other single factor.

Lack of encouragement for innovative teaching is also the norm for regular, tenured, or tenure-track faculty. This reality is reflected in some key findings from the latest survey of faculty attitudes and opinions by the Carnegie Foundation (Huber, 1997). Four survey items relate to innovative teaching, although none use that specific term. One item seeks reactions to the statement, "Interdisciplinary teaching is encouraged at my institution." Most faculty disagree or are neutral on this issue (9 percent strongly disagree, 20 percent disagree, and 22 percent are neutral, whereas 13 percent strongly agree, and 37 percent agree). Another item states, "Team teaching is encouraged at my institution." On this issue, two-thirds disagree or are neutral (15 percent strongly disagree, 26 percent somewhat disagree, and 25 percent are neutral, whereas 9 percent strongly agree, and 25 percent somewhat agree). A third item asks, "Do you ever supervise students in service learning activities off campus?" (57 percent of all faculty said "no"; 27 percent said "yes, occasionally"; and 17 percent said "yes, regularly"). The final item asks, "In your department, how much experimentation has there been with the use of technology in instruction?" Here 68 percent report "some" and 17 percent "a great deal." Naturally, responses vary among faculty at institutions typed as research, doctoral, master's, baccalaureate, and associate of arts, but the differences are much less than the similarities.

In sum, these items and others in the survey support our sense that most colleges and universities do not have a campus climate that encourages instructional innovation, and the metric of the credit hour is just a small part of the larger pattern. At research and doctoral universities particularly, but even at other campuses (apart from community colleges), research is favored over teaching in terms of rewards. At most community colleges and comprehensive universities, full-time faculty may be required to teach four or even five courses per semester, and they have little time to innovate, whatever their motivation. Striking exceptions are found, of course, in every category of institution and among faculty members on every campus.

More generally, regular faculty members—and even adjunct or part-time faculty—who truly want to innovate by infusing their courses with enhanced use of technology or in other ways can find the means to do so with the acquiescence if not encouragement of their department chairs and deans. But inertia, competing claims on time and attention, and lack of rewards are powerful forces pressing against innovation. In comparison, workload standards seem relatively modest barriers. Barriers to innovation are generally cumulative, however, and particularly in some public institutions, those relating to workload standards hinder instructional innovation.

Private Campuses

Currently at most private institutions, instructional workload is monitored and regulated by department chairs and deans without much more by way of guidance than such general norms as an expectation of two courses per semester. Even if standards for comparing faculty workload are maintained, they are not made public any more than individual faculty salaries are made public.

Henry Rosovsky, for a decade the dean of Harvard University, wryly reports in his 1990 book, *The University: An Owner's Manual,* that during his tenure, the average faculty course load at Harvard dropped from four to three, and he never authorized any change. For a more current view, we talked with administrators at a number of private campuses.

Typical comments came from one such administrator with overall charge of undergraduate education at a leading private research university who had also been an academic administrator at an elite liberal arts college. In essence, he said that he had no real notion of how instructional workload standards were set in the various departments of the four undergraduate schools that reported to him or at his former liberal arts college.

This administrator did know that department chairs negotiated directly with individual faculty members, with a general norm of two courses per semester being most common in the humanities, somewhat less in the social sciences, and one course per semester in the sciences. At his research university, as at most private campuses, the "course" is the metric used. The administrator said that at his institution, it is "expected" that a course will meet for three contact hours, although a faculty member might petition to change this norm. As an illustration, he cited an instance when he was a faculty member and successfully petitioned the school department and then curriculum committee to have a course meet for six hours per week and to count as the equivalent of two courses in terms of graduation standards and faculty instructional workload. Once a course is under way at this and most private institutions, little if any monitoring is done of the extent to which the course meets for the expected number of times per week or semester— except, of course, by students, who rarely complain if the actual number is less than expected.

The same administrator went on to say that faculty are able, indeed encouraged, to "buy out" of teaching one or more courses by attracting external research funding. When they do, their courses are usually taught by adjunct faculty. Released time is the coin of the academic realm, particularly at research universities. (This administrator told us that extended sabbaticals are another currency that can be used, particularly when there are pressures to avoid reducing teaching loads.) As a result, he said, few faculty are actually teaching two courses per semester as a regular practice. These comments were echoed with minor variations from other administrators at other private colleges and universities. At some of these campuses, credit hours were used, although at most, courses were the unit for describing faculty work.

Because most private institutions do not publish faculty workload standards, it was not possible to review a broad sample of those standards, and even those administrators with whom I talked did not want to comment for attribution. Based on these discussions, however, much anecdotal evidence suggests that the faculty reward system stifles innovation, particularly in the stress on research over teaching and in the pressures to gain released time from teaching.

Since the 1950s, especially at the most prestigious universities, both public and private, research excellence has been viewed as of primary importance in the ways faculty are rewarded—hiring, promotion, tenure, and compensation. This is particularly true at institutions known as "research" universities, but it is also the case at most others as well. (Community colleges, which are public, are an exception.) The emphasis on research has been fueled by federal government funding, which now totals more than $17 billion directed annually to institutions of higher education. An inevitable result has been a diminished focus on teaching, let alone innovative teaching.

We concluded, however, that neither faculty workload standards generally nor the credit-hour metric particularly could be isolated as a restraint on instructional innovation at private colleges and universities. Rather, our experience and the experience of those with whom we talked suggest that faculty members who want to innovate in their courses can do so on private campuses. If they do not, the reasons are more likely related to their own inertia to do something that is different and more time-consuming—at least initially—and the reality that innovation in teaching is rarely rewarded to the extent that is true for innovation in research.

Public Campuses

Every public institution of higher education needs some accounting system to keep track of faculty workload and to distribute teaching responsibilities among faculty members. The traditional approach has been to start with a set of norms, using "the course" as the base. This approach developed when virtually all courses involved lectures by a faculty member, usually for fifty-minute hours. The instruction norm was generally a number of courses per quarter or semester. The range among colleges and universities was from two courses or even fewer to five or even more.

At public institutions, however, particularly those that are not research universities, pressures often exist for equity among faculty members and for accountability from both administrators and external sources, such as legislatures and higher education commissions. At most public institutions, these pressures have led to some system of comparing faculty workload on a more fine-grained basis than number of courses. The student credit hour is the most common system.

In preparing this study, we reviewed some faculty workload standards available on the Internet. These suggest that the use of credit hours is particularly prevalent among large public colleges and universities—those awarding master's degrees, baccalaureate degrees, and associate's degrees—categories that cover the teaching of more than 80 percent of undergraduate students. In the public sector, some campuses state their expectations in terms of contact hours, but credit hours seem to be the more common standard.

The faculty senate of the University of Wisconsin campuses, for example, adopted a "faculty workload policy," which provides that "a full-time academic-year teaching load in the Department of History will be 24 student contact hours," and that "[t]his teaching load will include no more than 6 separate course preparations per year" (University of Wisconsin, 2003). Similarly, the policy of the City University of New York for 1996 through 2000, as expressed in the agreement between the university and its professional staff congress, states that professors at every level in the senior colleges hall have an annual teaching workload of twenty-one contact hours and twenty-seven contact hours in the community colleges (City University of New York, 2003).

The University of Hawaii, on the other hand, adopted a faculty workload policy of twenty-four semester credit hours per academic year at the four-year campuses and thirty semester credit hours at the community colleges (University of Hawaii, 2002). The University of Nebraska at Kearney has a faculty workload guideline of "eleven to thirteen hours per semester. However, a variety of circumstances may result in loads outside this range" (University of Nebraska, 2003). In addition, this university, like most whose policies we have reviewed, spells out the credit-hour equivalence of other instructional responsibilities. "Laboratory contact hours normally count as 1/2 of lecture contact hours." "Faculty assigned thirty student credit hours or more of independent studies in a given semester have their load reduced by three semester hours in that semester," and credit hours of thesis advising by faculty are doubled for purposes of computing student credit hours (University of Nebraska, 2003).

Whereas the published guidelines found at most public campuses seem to refer to either contact hours or, more commonly, credit hours, some, such as at the University of Alabama, College of Arts and Sciences, are stated only in hours. "The official workload of the university is 12 semester hours of teaching or equivalent service, during each term of the academic year" (University of Alabama, 2003).

At campuses where faculty are unionized, faculty workload is negotiated through collective bargaining. At some systems, such as the California state university system discussed below, the negotiated standards are stated with great specificity. At others, however, such as the State University of New York (SUNY), the system expectations are stated in general terms, and standards are set on each campus within the system.

We also reviewed some faculty workload standards that were adopted in a context of legislative efforts to enhance teaching as opposed to research. These often reflect a struggle between pressures to recognize faculty autonomy and those to encourage faculty attention to undergraduate teaching. The Ohio Board of Regents, for example, charged an advisory committee to develop faculty workload standards and guidelines. After an exhaustive process that must have been exhausting to the participants, that committee in 1994 produced a sixteen-page single-spaced document that shifts back and forth between these two poles for a dozen pages before stating that departments at campuses with baccalaureate, master's, and doctoral programs should have a norm of 50 to 60 percent of the total departmental workload devoted to teaching, but the percentage should be 80 to 90 percent at those with two-year or associate-degree programs (Ohio Board of Regents, 2003).

Modifying the Credit-Hour Approach

Nothing inherent in the credit-hour concept precludes a more calibrated metric than one class hour equals one credit hour for the purposes of faculty workload.

California State University. The California State University (CSU) adopted just such an approach when it moved in 1976 to a system of "weighted teaching units" (WTUs; Dumke, 1976). That system, modified in detail but not in approach, is still in place today, and it serves as an example of both the advantages and the limitations of a more calibrated metric. Each CSU campus has its own rules and regulations regarding WTUs, but they are essentially minor variations on a major theme. The new campus at Monterey Bay (see Chapter Three) has proposed a somewhat different approach to the WTUs, involving individual faculty WTU contracts with the campus administration, but the core concept is the same.

At CSU, the normal workload of a full-time faculty member consists of two components, as stated in the policies and procedures adopted by the system trustees in 1976:

—12 weighted teaching units (WTU) of direct instructional assignments, including classroom and laboratory instruction and instructional supervision (such as student thesis, project, or intern supervision) equivalent to thirty-six hours per week

—3 WTU equivalencies of indirect instructional activity such as student advisement, curriculum development and improvements, and committee assignments (four to nine hours per week) [p. 1].

Under the system, each course is given what is called a K factor, ranging from 1.0 to 6.0. Large lecture classes with forty-five or fewer students have a K factor of 1.0, many laboratories in other than science areas have a K factor of 1.3, laboratories in foreign languages have a K factor of 1.5, science laboratories have a K factor of 2.0, production courses in music and journalism have a K factor of 3.0, and coaching major intercollegiate sports has a K factor of 6.0. A course is designated with a number of units based on how many times it meets; that number is then multiplied by the K factor to determine how many WTUs a faculty member receives for teaching the course. A three-unit course with a K factor of 1.0 receives three WTUs, and a three-unit course with a K factor of 2.0 receives six WTUs. A faculty member is expected to engage in a total of twelve WTUs at any one time. It is assumed that a faculty member will be engaging in three WTUs of advising and committee work, which are counted toward the needed total of twelve. The original CSU policies and procedures state that "[t]hus Weighted Teaching Units are a measure of the weekly rate of faculty effort" (Dumke, 1976, p. 1).

The WTU system was originally designed to help shape budgets. The WTU formula was designed as a means for each campus in the CSU system to organize its financial needs. The formula determined the campus budget and its request for funds to the CSU central office and the legislature. A course with more than forty-five students—even one more student—would receive double the number of WTUs as the same course with fewer than forty-five students, so a campus would strive to have more than forty-five students in the course and the budget that came with those students.

About a decade ago, CSU switched to "dollar-based budgeting," which means that each campus receives a single allocation of funds to spend as its administration allocates. However, CSU has had faculty unions that bargain collectively at the statewide, rather than campuswide, level for almost thirty years. Perhaps as a result of statewide bargaining, the WTU system has remained essentially unchanged. From the perspective of the union leadership, it serves as a means to ensure that campus administrations do not impose too heavy workloads on the faculty. Further, campuses are still required to submit faculty workforce reports to the CSU central office, and deans use these in negotiating with campus presidents.

The obvious advantages of the WTU system, or some other modification of the credit hour so that a multiplier is used, include an ability to measure faculty workload in ways that take account of variations in number of students, degree of student supervision, and other variables. Problems arise, however, at least in the system as it has developed at CSU. An example is when two faculty members teach the same course (Psychology 200, for example), and one wants a field component or to teach the course on-line and the other wants to offer a straight lecture course.

More troublesome, the system has no obvious way to deal with on-line courses, except on an ad hoc basis. There is a category, naturally, of "courses that do not fit into any of the usual classifications." This category apparently is used when there are problems. But this default approach is not adequate to handle the exploding number of on-line courses. As a result, the system discourages this innovative mode. Informal discussions with administrators at the CSU campus in San Francisco indicate that this is an example of a larger problem—the inability of the WTU to deal appropriately with innovations in teaching as a matter of faculty workload. The consequence is to discourage innovations, just as we had hypothesized.

University of Texas. The University of Texas has adopted another variant. Classes of more than sixty students are multiplied by a "weighing factor" that increases by 0.1 per ten students up to ninety-nine students, and 0.1 for each twenty-five students from 100 to 250 students. Other equivalencies are also specified for purposes such as administrative assignments and new course development. Again, however, there seems to be an inherent bias in the system against innovation.

Miami-Dade Community Colleges. In the late 1960s, Miami-Dade Community Colleges dropped the term *student credit hour* and since then have referred only to "credits." The former president of the system, Robert McCabe, thinks that the most important single step that higher education could take in this area would be to follow this approach. Such a step would enable a focus on learning, he argues, rather than on hours.

The Miami-Dade Community Colleges system has a point system that works in the following way. Each faculty full-time equivalent needs to generate sixty points. The norm is that one hour of lecture earns four points. A faculty member who teaches five courses that each meet three hours per week for a semester earns sixty points. Points are also awarded for supervising students, conducting labs, sitting on committees, and other tasks. Over time, the necessary translations have been worked out, and even though there is now a faculty union at Miami-Dade Community Colleges, the system continues.

The Future: A Fundamental Shift?

Dennis Jones and his colleagues at the National Center on Higher Education Research are thoughtful commentators on higher education. They have suggested that a fundamental shift may be under way in the realm of faculty workload, a shift that cannot be accommodated by the credit-hour metric, at least without significant modification.

Jones argues that as long as the standard mode of instructional delivery was the lecture for fifty minutes, any metric could have worked for faculty workload (as opposed to student learning). In fact, the course was the dominant metric in most private institutions, and it still is. But the credit hour worked fine for this standard mode as well, and dominated in public institutions.

Long ago, however, Jones points out, research universities and their administrators realized that faculty needed some help when classes were larger than a certain size and particularly when labs were involved. That help came in the form of teaching assistants, who took over small sections, the labs, and sometimes the lectures and the assessments (most often examinations).

The course or credit hour, Jones contends, did well enough, even at research universities, when the only variables were class size and labs or other out-of-class experiences. He believes, however, that there may be a quiet revolution going on in breaking the elements of instruction into component parts. These components include design, development, delivery, mentoring, and assessment. A senior faculty person may now be responsible for design and development, an adjunct faculty person for delivery, a teaching assistant on the Internet for mentoring, and a computer program for assessment.

The credit hour, or even the "course," cannot keep up with this level of change, Jones contends. "Standard" courses are increasingly becoming nonstandard. It is no longer possible, Jones argues, to tweak the credit hour to handle this fractionation of instructional authority and responsibility. That is why the "new new" institutions, such as the University of Phoenix (see Chapter Three), have recognized this reality and judge faculty instructional workload in pieces. About 8,000 "practitioner faculty" teach most of the courses at that university, but only 250 teach full-time. The practitioner faculty are generally paid on a per-course basis, and when they attend faculty-training meetings or have other responsibilities, they are paid additionally. The university has a "virtual writing lab," for example, and practitioner faculty who advise students on their writing via the Internet are also paid on a piece basis.

Does all this suggest that the credit hour is an impediment to innovation in terms of faculty workload? Not quite, or at least that is not the most accurate way to frame the problem, as Jones views it. The problem, rather, is that as long as the definition of faculty workload is stated in terms of class size—so that, for example, twenty-five students meeting three times per week is one course or three credit hours, and the total load is four courses or twelve credit hours, a faculty member has no incentive to do other than get twenty-six students in her class so that it counts as two courses. More troubling, the institution has no incentive to use technology because that only makes sense with economies of scale, and if twenty-five students are the measure of a class, then that is the measure faculty will use. This is exactly what happens at CSU, for example, where every use of on-line instruction is an ad hoc decision, with an entrenched bureaucracy guarding the revised credit-hour metric.

Conclusions

Workload regulations generally, or the credit-hour metric particularly viewed alone, were not found to be stifling innovation. We did conclude, however, that at some public campuses, particularly ones with faculty unions, those regulations—in combination with other factors—made innovation more difficult. On those campuses, the credit-hour metric and its various modifications contribute to an environment that does not reward instructional innovations but, rather, makes them more challenging to implement. The credit hour is thus part of a larger system of courses and credits that makes innovation more difficult. As Bob Schoenberg, a wise commentator and expert on innovations in faculty rewards, puts the point, the credit hours are part of the larger framework that is so convenient a measure of faculty effort that it further entrenches the system of credits and courses. This system impedes instructional innovation. It could be that the system will be forced to change, along the lines suggested by Jones. But this review suggests that the forces of inertia are powerful and will be hard to overcome.

References

City University of New York. "1996–2000 CUNY-PSC Agreement." [http://www1.cuny. edu/cuny-psc/toc2.html]. 2003.

Dumke, G. S. "Consolidation of Faculty Workload Materials." Memorandum to CSU Presidents, Aug. 16, 1976.

Huber, M. T. *Community College Faculty Attitudes and Trends.* Stanford, Calif.: National Center for Postsecondary Education, Stanford University, 1997.

Ohio Board of Regents. *Faculty Workload.* [http://www.regents.state.oh.us/plandocs/ worklad.htm/]. 2003.

Rosovsky, H. *The University: An Owner's Manual.* New York: Norton, 1990.

University of Alabama. *Faculty Manual: Workload.* [http://www.as.ua.edu/as/faculty/man-ual/policies/workload.html]. 2003.

University of Hawaii Board of Regents. *By-Laws and Policies, Sections 9–16.* [http:// www/Hawaii.edu/svpa/ed/e1202.pdf]. 2002.

University of Nebraska at Kearney. *Faculty Workload Guidelines.* [http://aaunk.edu/fac-ultyhandbook/wkldtoc.htm]. 2003.

University of Wisconsin, Department of History. *Faculty Workload Policy.* [http://wash-ington.uwc.edu/academics/depts/history/workload40.htm]. 2003.

THOMAS EHRLICH is a senior scholar at the Carnegie Foundation for the Advancement of Teaching.

5

Accreditation, the process of peer review to ensure the quality of a degree program, has depended on institutions measuring degree content in student credit hours.

Accreditation and the Credit Hour

Jane V. Wellman

In this chapter, I review the role that accreditation plays in defining and enforcing the credit-hour measure. Research for this background chapter is based on a review of the accreditation standards for a sample of accrediting agencies: all eight of the regional agencies, five national accreditors, and nine specialized agencies. The goal of this part of the research has been to reach a general characterization of the role of accreditation in certifying, defining, and enforcing credit hour measures. It is not intended to be a critical analysis of the effectiveness of accreditation or a comprehensive discussion about the ways that accreditation helps to ensure quality in American higher education. Also, the research is not exhaustive because standards for all agencies have not been reviewed, nor were institutional representatives interviewed about their experiences with accrediting agencies. Many of the agencies are rewriting their standards through consultative processes that may be attempting to move past the credit hour. Nonetheless, the results are sufficiently revealing about at least the past role of accreditation to answer the core research questions of the study.

Background on Accreditation

Accreditation is the external peer review and certification of academic quality in higher education in the United States. It serves three purposes: public certification of minimum or threshold standards of quality, a framework for institutional self-assessment and continuous improvement, and a requirement for institutions to receive certain funds (such as federal financial aid) or to enable their graduates to sit for state licensing examinations. Accreditation thus plays a dual role of promoting internal quality improvement and a quasi-regulatory role of external quality assessment. Accreditation can be applied to entire institutions or to schools (such as law schools), programs (teacher education), or units (hospitals) within institutions. Accreditation of higher education is a distinctively American invention, substituting for direct governmental regulation of academic standards such as that performed by central governments elsewhere. It is a quasi-regulatory, nongovernmental activity, although regulated by the federal government. (For more on this topic, see Chapter Six on the federal regulatory role and the credit hour.)

The accreditation process requires institutions or programs to take several steps before applying for accreditation. The first step is to establish eligibility to apply for accreditation by meeting the agency's eligibility standards—a quality prescreening before agencies agree to accept an institution for a full-blown accreditation review. As an example, all agencies maintain eligibility standards that require institutions or programs to be state licensed and to have education as their primary purpose. The regional accreditors also require institutions to be degree granting and to have a governance structure that ensures academic integrity and a faculty with appropriate credentials for the program. Once an institution establishes eligibility for review, it must prepare a comprehensive self-assessment using agency review standards and submit to an on-site review by a team of peer reviewers. The visiting team reports its assessment of the institution's status; final decisions on accreditation are made by the accreditation commission. The accreditation review cycle typically lasts around five years; some agencies allow longer periods between reviews, with shorter review cycles for institutions being monitored or on probation.

Types of Accreditation

There are three types of accreditation: regional, national, and specialized. The terms refer to the scope of degree or certificate authority recognized for that agency by the U.S. Department of Education: regional agencies may accredit institutions only within specified geographic areas, national agencies may accredit institutions anywhere in the nation, and specialized agencies are confined to particular fields. Regional and national accreditation both are granted for entire institutions, whereas specialized accreditation is provided for specific programs or fields, usually in the professions. Most institutions have dual accreditation, both for individual schools or programs by specialized agencies and from a regional or national agency.

Regional Accreditation. Regional accreditation is the largest and historically the oldest form of accreditation; it is most often sought by nonprofit and public, degree-granting institutions. There are eight agencies in six regions (both New England and Western maintain separate agencies for junior and technical colleges) that together accredit roughly three thousand institutions enrolling close to fourteen million students.

National Accreditation. National accreditation is an alternative to regional accreditation and is usually sought by trade, business, and technical schools in the for-profit sector. (Several national agencies accredit religious schools that do not fit the vocational for-profit model: the American Association of Bible Colleges, the Association of Advanced Rabbinical and Talmudic Schools, the Association of Theologic Schools, and the Transnational Association of Christian Colleges and Schools. These agencies are classified as "national" because they accredit entire institutions and have national jurisdiction, but their focus is more typical of a specialized agency.) Eleven national agencies collectively accredit 3,564 institutions enrolling around 4.75 million students. The two largest national agencies by student enrollments are the Distance Education and Training Council, which oversees about fifty-three institutions serving three million students, and the Accrediting Council for Continuing Education and Training, which oversees noncollegiate continuing education programs. Key differences between the national and regional accreditation standards lie in governance and curriculum. Regional standards circumscribe faculty autonomy on matters of curriculum and standards, whereas national standards give the institutional governing boards greater corporate decision-making authority. The regional standards also require some kind of general education for the baccalaureate degree, something not always true for the national agencies.

Specialized Agencies. Specialized agencies accredit individual schools or programs within larger colleges and universities. There are about sixty individual specialized agencies whose fields range from medicine, law, engineering, and teacher education to culinary arts, construction, music, dance, forestry, and allied health. In many areas, such as architecture, accounting, and teacher education, state licensing laws require candidates for state licenses to have graduated from schools accredited by the relevant specialized agency. As a result, many of these forms of specialized accreditation have a stronger direct connection to governmental regulation than the other kinds of accreditation.

Review of Standards

Standards and eligibility criteria were reviewed for all eight regional accreditors and for four national and nine specialized agencies. The national and specialized agencies were selected because they represent some of the oldest and most established of such agencies, thus touching the majority of institutions of higher education.

All of the ways that the credit hour might be defined and enforced were considered: standards on academic credits, definitions, and measures of the credit hour; policies for awarding of credit for education offered outside the institution (either by transfer of credit, through testing, experiential education, or other kinds of assessments); number of credits required for a degree or certificate; admissions standards related to credit; standards for minimum credits in general education; and residency requirements for the awarding of credit. Measures of time that might be surrogates for some dimensions of the credit hour were also looked at, such as standards for academic calendars and definitions of *full-time* for either students or faculty. The goal was to identify broad patterns and common definitions—not a comparative analysis of agency standards—that can help answer the research questions about the enforcement of the credit hour by accrediting agencies. Also, is this role a barrier to academic reform or does it provide an external validation or audit to ensure consistency in the application of the credit hour between and within institutions?

Distinct patterns were found among the regional, national, and specialized agencies. All require learning to be codified in some way, either through credit units (in degree-granting institutions), clock hours (in non-degree-granting institutions), or continuing education units (noncredit courses such as adult education). Agencies that accredit degree-granting programs require credit unit measures, clock hours are used for some non-degree and certificate courses—cosmetology, for example—and continuing education units are used for noncollegiate adult education such as English as a second language or union-related classes. Specialized agencies, in contrast to the regional and national agencies, may refer to credit hours, but their standards typically (but not always) downplay the credit and focus instead on knowledge and skill development obtained through whole learning sequences, including courses, service learning, internships, and other practicums.

Regional Standards. The regional accrediting agencies, which are responsible for the institutional accreditation of most public and private not-for-profit colleges, are for the most part vague about the definition of the measure of academic credits. This ambiguity is probably attributable to the wide range of institutions seeking regional accreditation and a stronger emphasis on institutional improvement and self-assessment than on meeting threshold standards. The standards seem to be a framework for assessment rather than a distinct set of performance standards that must be met. Nonetheless, regional accrediting standards cannot be looked to to reveal either the qualitative or quantitative basis for the measurement of student learning in academic credits. A few agencies maintain glossaries of terms that are attached to standards where the student credit hour is defined in terms of "time on task":

> A credit unit is a quantification of academic learning. One semester unit represents how much time a typical student is expected to devote to learning in one week of full-time undergraduate study (at least 40 to 45 hours including class time and preparation). Thus a six-week summer session might, if full-time, equate to six units. An alternative norm is one unit for three hours of student work per week ([for example], one hour of lecture and two of study or three of laboratory) for ten weeks per quarter or 15 weeks per semester. A full-time undergraduate student program should normally be 14 to 16 units, and if full-time, no less than 12 units. More time is expected to be devoted to

study at the graduate level, typically more than three hours of study for every hour in class. A full-time graduate program is normally nine units or less [Western Association of Schools and Colleges, 2001, p. 121].

This definition is published separately from the actual standards for student learning, which do not mention time on task but rather institutional purpose, degree programs, learning outcomes, and faculty decision-making authority.
Some other examples follow:

All degrees—undergraduate and graduate—awarded by the institution are clearly defined in terms of levels of student achievement necessary for graduation that represent more than simply an accumulation of courses or credits [Western Association of Schools and Colleges, 2001, p. 20].

The institution has the responsibility for the academic elements of all instructional programs and courses for which it offers institutional credit, including. . . . course content and the delivery of the instructional program and the approval of faculty; admission, registration and retention of students; evaluation of prior learning; and evaluation of student progress, including the awarding and recording of credit [New England Association of Schools and Colleges, Commission on Colleges, 2001].

The Commission expects an affiliated institution to be able to equate its learning experiences with semester or quarter credit hours using practices common to institutions of higher education, to justify the lengths of its programs in comparison to similar programs found in accredited institutions of higher education, and to justify any program-specific tuition in terms of program costs, program length, and program objectives. Affiliated institutions notify the Commission of any significant changes in the relationships among credits, program length, and tuition [North Central Association of Schools and Colleges, Higher Learning Commission, 2001].

The North Central Commission on Higher Education has often been the first of the regional agencies to accredit some types of nontraditional institutions, including the University of Phoenix and the Jones International University, and was jointly involved in the review of the application from Western Governors' University, with several other regional associations. In 2001 it was renamed the Commission on Higher Learning to advertise its increased emphasis on accreditation based on assessment and quality improvement of student learning. The North Central agency also added a new element to its standard on credit, which is that "faculty have and exercise responsibility for determining the institution's award of academic credit" (2002). The new clarification about the basis for awarding student credits suggests that the commission is less interested in measuring conventional, institution-based measures of time and location as criteria for student credit than in knowing that decisions about what constitutes academic credit are made by the faculty.

Most of the regional accreditation agencies specify the minimum number of credit units required for the baccalaureate degree: 120 semester hours or 180 quarter hours. Alternative routes for achieving credits other than by taking courses at the institution are permitted, and the standards go into some detail about procedures for determining credit for transfer students, through portfolio assessments of experiential education, or other kinds of achieved learning assessments. These alternative routes help to amplify the underlying values of quality latent in the standards. For instance, the Western Association of Schools and Colleges, Senior College Commission, permits credit for prior experiential learning only at the undergraduate level and for no more than thirty semester units toward the degree. It also requires that the evaluation of experiential learning relate to the theories and data of the field and be evaluated by a qualified faculty member. The Middle States Association of Schools and Colleges' (2002) policies are similar: "Recognition of college-level learning derived from work or other life experience may facilitate a student's progress without compromising an institution's integrity or the quality of its degrees. An institution's policies and procedures should provide appropriate consideration, consistent with good educational practice, for the individual student who has gained college level learning from other sources. However, procedures to assess learning for the award of academic credit (especially where such credit is part of an accelerated degree program) should define college level learning and state clearly that credit is awarded for demonstrated learning and not merely experience" (p. 42).

In all the regional agencies, requirements for graduate degrees are typically not expressed in unit expectations. Rather, graduate degree requirements speak to a body of work that must be accomplished and the expected relationship of the student to the program. For instance, most standards for graduate programs have residency requirements that require that the majority (usually two-thirds) of units be taken at the institution awarding the degree. Only one agency (Southern Association of Colleges and Schools) maintains residency requirements for the baccalaureate degree: at least 25 percent of semester credit hours must be earned through the institution awarding the degree. All of the agencies have similar policies on procedures for review of credit transfer, stressing that transfer decisions should be based on course equivalency and applicability review, conducted by the faculty of the institution pursuant to its mission.

Standards of definition for academic calendars are another way that accrediting agencies convey expectations for "time on learning." Most provide general guidelines for academic calendars, by defining the standard terms for semesters (seventeen weeks, with at least fifteen weeks of regularly scheduled classes) or quarters (a range of ten to fifteen weeks), but provide a good deal of leeway for alternative calendars. The criteria for acceptance of nontraditional calendars again reveal the tone of the context for the standards. The standard of the Southern Association of Colleges and Schools (2001), for example, specifies that

> Undergraduate courses offered in non-traditional formats, [for example], concentrated or abbreviated time periods, must be designed to ensure an opportunity for preparation, reflection and analysis concerning the subject matter. At least one calendar week of reflection and analysis should be provided to students for each semester hour, or equivalent quarter hours, or undergraduate credit awarded. The institution must demonstrate that students completing these programs or courses have acquired equivalent levels of knowledge and competencies to those acquired in traditional formats [p. 30].

National Agencies. Review of the national accrediting agency standards found them to be more precise with respect to definitions and calculations of student learning than those of the regional agencies, with a fairly in-depth formula for credit hours. Some of this focus on time may occur because the national agencies often accredit nondegree certificate or noncredit programs, which by federal law must count student learning in clock hours (for credit-bearing courses) or continuing education units rather than in credit hours. Perhaps because the national accrediting agencies oversee all ways to record learning, they focus more on explaining the measures and how they relate to each other. The national agencies also typically accredit institutions that specialize in relatively few programs or disciplines, such as business, accounting, or technology certification. Greater focus on vocational and professional programs designed to prepare students for particular occupations may be another reason standards are more specific. The following types of definitions were found:

> One quarter credit hours equals, at a minimum, 10 classroom hours of lecture, 20 hours of laboratory, and 30 hours of practicum. . . . or. . . . one semester credit hour equals, at a minimum, 15 classroom hours of lecture, 30 hours of laboratory, and 45 hours of practicum [Council on Occupational Education, 2002, p. G14].

> The definition of a "clock (contact) hour" states that the minimum instructional time is 50 minutes of supervised or directed instruction and appropriate break(s). Therefore, when calculating conversions from clock to credit hours or allocating credit for courses, institutions must take great care to ensure that scheduled breaks are educationally appropriate. Long periods of instruction with unusually short or no breaks are not acceptable. The institution has the burden of convincing the Council that the breaks are sufficiently long and frequent for the program being taught. Thus, it is rare for an institution to be able to divide by 50 in calculating the credit-hour equivalent of contact hours; usually, the denominator should be 60 or something

between 50 and 60 [Accrediting Council for Independent Schools and Colleges, 2003, p. G14].

National standards do not show the same degree of deference as those of the regional agencies to the role of faculty in determining the basis for credit awards. The national standards require a greater degree of oversight and approval of institutional decisions by the accrediting agency. For instance, the policy on credit award for nontraditional courses for the Accrediting Council for Independent Schools and Colleges (2003) states:

> Credit award rationales for nontraditional delivery of courses or programs ([for example], distance education, collaborative learning, or independent study) generally do not use the above lecture/laboratory/practicum formulas for credit calculation. The rationale used must be submitted to the Council for pre-approval of the credit calculation. As a part of the approval application, an institution must demonstrate that the clock or credit hours awarded are appropriate for the degrees and credentials offered using a thoroughly developed rationale. The institution may accomplish this by demonstrating that students completing these programs or courses have acquired equivalent levels of knowledge, skills, or competencies to those acquired in traditional formats. Courses offered in nontraditional formats must be structured to ensure that students have sufficient opportunity for preparation, reflection, and analysis concerning learned subject matter. Institutions should be aware that federal law requires a minimum number of weeks per academic year [p. G14].

There is some evidence in the national standards that these agencies audit the basis for awarding credit and clock hours more than the regional agencies. This degree of oversight may be the result of U.S. Department of Education scrutiny of inflated academic calendars among some of the for-profit institutions. The Accrediting Council for Independent Schools and Colleges, for instance, collects data from its institutions to determine national averages for program lengths, tuition, and fees. Its standards state that institutions with program lengths more than one standard deviation from the average will be required to submit an explanation for the deviation. The attentiveness to federal regulations is also evident in the accrediting standards for "satisfactory academic progress"—standards specific about academic achievement and normal rates of progress. They provide a detailed formula for calculating academic and student attrition based on student credit hours or clock hours attempted versus those that are completed. The issue of satisfactory academic progress became an issue of contention between many of the for-profit institutions and the Department of Education in the late 1980s and 1990s, when rising default rates on student loans and institutional closures caused concern about institutional integrity in the sector.

Specialized. The standards for the specialized agencies reviewed are different from either the regional or national standards. Whereas the regional standards are general and the national standards detailed and formulaic, the specialized agencies define development obtained through course sequences within an established curriculum in terms of skill and knowledge. The reason lies in the basic differences between institutional and specialized accreditation: the latter is oriented to discrete subject areas and professional practice. Specialized agencies also typically concentrate on programs or schools within larger colleges or universities that have institutional accreditation, so the focus is only on the relevant specific discipline or body of work. Most include some practical experience or clinical training as part of their degree requirements, and these are similarly framed in terms of skills and competencies and overall time on task rather than in units.

As most of these agencies accredit programs that prepare professionals to sit for licensure examinations, an external assessment of student knowledge and skills is common. Some of the requirements for licensure may complement the accreditation requirements, so specific requirements for time, credits, or knowledge, might well be found in licensure rather than accreditation requirements. State licensure laws for these professions were not reviewed, so there is no information on how this trade-off operates in practice.

In almost all of the specialized agencies reviewed, the standards for degree or certificate attainment are related to student skill development and learning expectations necessary for practice of the profession. Time requirements for the degree are typically expressed in years, not credits. Typically, there is much more detail about the curriculum content and the required types of courses, although most agencies allow leeway for institutional faculty to determine specific course titles. In medical education, for instance, the curriculum is framed as sequences of courses and years leading to student internship and residencies. The requirements for dental education similarly balance years of required course work with mandatory practical training.

In a few of the specialized agencies, there is some evidence of standards being rewritten in the past decade to focus on evidence of skills, knowledge, and ability rather than course sequences and curriculum standards. The National League of Nursing Accreditation Commission (2001), the National Council for the Accreditation of Teacher Education (2002), and the Accreditation Board for Engineering and Technology (2001) all focus on expected student learning outcomes, framed as knowledge, skills, and abilities. Their standards dwell much more on ways for the programs to assess how effective they are in meeting these expectations than on how results are achieved. Nonetheless, they usually require a minimum amount of time to be spent in the program acquiring these skills and competencies. The American Bar Association (accreditor for law programs) is an exception.

The American Bar Association's standards (2002) are detailed and pre-scriptive with respect to credit hour and time requirements needed to obtain the degree. The standards, currently being revised to allow greater flexibil-ity for distance learning, are precise with regard to time-based measures of learning: they apply to schools, which must maintain academic calendars of 130 days and eight calendar months (excluding time for reading periods or examinations); degree standards (fifty-six thousand minutes of instruc-tion time excluding out-of-class study); time on study standards (to receive credit for a semester, students must be enrolled at least eight semester hours and may not be employed more than twenty hours per week); and atten-dance (regular and punctual class attendance is necessary to satisfy resi-dence credit-hour standards, and institutions are audited on their procedures for taking and recording attendance). At least forty-five thou-sand of the fifty-six thousand minutes shall be in courses in residence in the law school. The fifty-six thousand-minute standard is maintained even though the standards are being revised to provide greater leeway for dis-tance learning.

Summary and Conclusions

All of the accreditation agencies require degree- and certificate-bound learn-ing to be measured in some way, through either credit, clock, continuing education, or course measures. There are some significant variations among agencies in the degree of specificity about how learning units are to be mea-sured. Regional agency standards typically do not define what credit units or hours are or how they should be measured or audited, although all of the regional agencies require learning to be measured in credits. Requirements that equate learning with time-based measures are embedded in some of the regional standards—for instance, in criteria on units required for degrees—or academic calendars. For the most part, regional accreditation standards leave it to the institution and specifically to the faculty in the institutions to determine the appropriate basis for the awarding of credit. The regional standards focus on a review of the institutional policies for awarding credit, to ensure that their policies are clearly stated and consistently enforced, rather than on direct regulation of the basis for credits themselves. They also provide more details about what might be called alternative routes for the awarding of academic credit, such as the acceptance of transfer credits, credit by examination, portfolio assessment of student learning, and resi-dency requirements for degrees.

The national agency standards, on the other hand, more often mention specific measures of the basis for credit determination, and time-based mea-sures are more common. The standards are technical and formulaic and sug-gest that the basis for unit determinations and academic calendars are reviewed and audited by the agencies. The national standards do not evince the same kind of deference to institutional autonomy and faculty decision making as the regional standards. National agencies also seem to be auditing their institutions about credit- and clock-hour policies and even provide their institutions with feedback about how their policies relate to those in place in other agencies.

Of the three types of agencies, the specialized accrediting agency standards generally make the least mention of credit units. They are framed holistically in terms of broad bands of knowledge, competencies, and sequences of learning experiences rather than in units. Several of the specialized agencies seem to have gone far in focusing on demonstrated effectiveness in skill and knowledge development as the basis for quality assurance. Their tasks in doing this may be easier than would be the case for regional agencies because of their narrower focus on a field of professional study. They also have their learning validated through external licensing examinations of graduates. Not all of the specialized agencies that were reviewed have moved in this direction; the American Bar Association's standards in particular are clearly committed to a specific, time-based standard.

In evaluating what this analysis means in terms of the project's research hypotheses, a particular interest was to understand if external oversight of the credit hour by accrediting agencies either provides a layer of external validation to the credit-hour system or becomes a barrier to academic reform. The answer is a qualified no. Regional accrediting agencies are the most flexible in their approach to assessing and enforcing credit-hour measures, and their standards do not seem to be barriers to innovation in teaching or learning. However, they offer little guidance to their institutions on the basis for validating academic credit other than in measures of time on learning, and the detailed formulas that appear in agency glossaries suggest that the more rigid formulations of time-based standards might be enforced. As a result, institutions or programs anxious about their accreditation status might be loath to move too aggressively away from an auditable, time-based credit formulation. The regional agencies also appear to be conducting little oversight about the basis for awarding of credit hours in conventional classroom-based instruction, so disparities between disciplines or institutions in the criteria for assigning credit hours would not be routinely audited by these accreditors. And, because some of the specialized accreditors still enforce time-based measures, this means that there are differences within institutions according to the programs that have specialized accreditation. This may inhibit institutions from implementing comprehensive change because of the difficulties of maintaining different standards (for instance, in instructional calendars) among different programs or academic divisions.

The specialized agencies present a different and more mixed picture. Several of them—notably the National Council for Accreditation of Teacher Education, the National League of Nursing Accreditation Commission, and the Accreditation Board for Engineering and Technology—are clearly focused on learning outcomes rather than time-based measures. Their standards go into detail about alternative ways for programs to demonstrate teaching effectiveness. The fact that they all have an external licensure examination that serves as a way of validating their success may be one of the factors helping them to move in this direction. At the other end of the continuum, the American Bar Association retains prescriptive time-based measures for learning. Alone among the agencies reviewed, it offers no guidance to institutions wishing to experiment with alternative approaches to teaching and learning.

The national agencies present a different picture from either the regional or specialized agencies. They maintain detailed formulas about the basis for awarding academic credit, and their standards suggest that they audit institutions to ensure that they are conforming and awarding academic credit appropriately. The reason for their more aggressive enforcement of the standard probably lies in their history of some nationally accredited institutions running afoul of the federal government in audits of fraud in the student aid program. The national agencies also frequently accredit institutions that do not award credit for degrees but instead measure learning in clock hours or continuing education units. Because their institutions must juggle these different metrics for recording learning, they may be more attentive to ensuring that time-based standards are applied equitably.

References

Accreditation Board for Engineering and Technology. *Accreditation Policy and Procedure Manual*. [http://www.abet.org/images/2002.03APPM.pdf]. Nov. 2001.

Accrediting Council for Independent Schools and Colleges. *Accreditation Criteria*. [http://www.acics.org/content.cfm?L1=2&L2=6.0]. Jan. 2003.

American Bar Association. *Standards for Approval of Law Schools*. [http://www.abanet.org/legaled]. 2002.

Council on Occupational Education. *Accreditation Handbook*. [http://www.council.org/Documents/Publications/Handbook/2002_coe_handbook.pdf]. 2002.

Middle States Association of Schools and Colleges. *Characteristics of Excellence in Higher Education: Standards for Accreditation*. [http://www.msache.org/characteristics%20book.pdf]. 2002.

National Council for the Accreditation of Teacher Education. *Professional Standards for the Accreditation of Schools, Colleges and Departments of Education*. Washington, D.C.: National Council for the Accreditation of Teacher Education, 2002.

National League of Nursing Accreditation Commission. *Accreditation Manual and Interpretive Guidelines by Program Type*. [http://www.nlnac.org/Manual%20&%201G/01_accreditation_manual.htm]. 2001.

New England Association of Schools and Colleges, Commission on Colleges. *Standards of Accreditation*. [http://www.neasc.org/cihe/stancihe.htm]. 2001.

North Central Association of Schools and Colleges, Higher Learning Commission. *Criteria for Accreditation*. [http://www.ncahigherlearningcommission.org/resources/policies/edinstia.html#1a]. Feb. 2001.

North Central Commission on Higher Education. *Criteria for Accreditation and General Institutional Requirements*. Feb. 2002.

Southern Association of Colleges and Schools, Commission on Colleges. *Principles of Accreditation.* [http://www.sacscoc.org/pdf/Proposed%20Principles%20of%20 Accreditation.pdf]. Dec. 2001.
Western Association of Schools and Colleges. *Handbook of Accreditation.* [http:// www.wascweb.org/senior/handbook.pdf]. 2001.

JANE V. WELLMAN *is a senior associate with the Institute for Higher Education Policy in Washington, D.C.*

*The expansion of federal financial aid programs means
that in the past twenty years, the federal government has
become the biggest single regulator of the student credit
hour as a time-based measure. Yet, the federal
government shows interest in moving away from focusing
on administrative and financial matters to issues of
academic policy and quality.*

Of Time and the Feds: The Federal Interest in Enforcing the Credit Hour

Jane V. Wellman

This chapter summarizes current research on the role of the federal government in defining or enforcing (or both) the credit-hour measure in higher education, focusing on the role played by the U.S. Department of Education (USDE) in shaping the credit-hour system. Federal influence on higher education goes well beyond the USDE because of its roles in research, environmental and civil rights laws, and through the tax system. Other agencies also use the credit hour or derivative measures in their work, but the USDE is the agency with program administration, funding, and reporting responsibilities that permeate all of higher education. Its definitions and use of the credit hour are subsequently adopted by other agencies. It also has by far the strongest policy role among federal agencies with respect to institutions of higher education.

Role of USDE in Higher Education

The USDE is the smallest and the youngest of the cabinet-level agencies. The federal role in higher education preceded the creation of the USDE, with the post-World War II GI Bill that gave returning servicemen and women a voucher for postsecondary education. USDE, created in 1972 during the Carter Administration, took its staff and programs from the division of education within the old Department of Health, Education, and Welfare. The authorizing legislation states that the department's purpose is "to ensure equal access and promote educational excellence" in U.S. education (20 U.S.C., Chapter 31, Section 1228 [a]). The federal role historically has been confined to the administration of "pass-through" funding to states and school districts for programs designed to promote equal educational opportunity and improvements in quality. Unlike national governments elsewhere in the world, USDE does not have a standard-setting role either in K-12 or higher education. In fact, the authorizing legislation for USDE explicitly constrains any policy control over education. The law states,

> No provision of any applicable program shall be construed to authorize any department, agency, officer, or employee of the United States to exercise any direction, supervision, or control over the curriculum, program of instruction, administration, or personnel of any educational institution, school, or school system, or over the selection of library resources, textbooks, or other printed or published instructional materials by any educational institution or school system [20 U.S.C., Chapter 31, Section 1232].

Despite this statutory prohibition, the line between the federal interest in equal opportunity and promoting excellence and "direction, supervision, and control" over educational curriculum and administration is not always easy to draw. Over the years, Congress has assigned incrementally greater policy authority to USDE in elementary and secondary education as well as in higher education. The strengthened federal educational policy role has grown in the K–12 arena, especially after the 1983 publication of the *Nation at Risk* report (National Commission on Excellence in Education, 1983), which set the stage for a national educational reform movement. First in the "Goals 2000" legislation and more recently in the "No Child Left Behind" law of 2001, the federal government has moved to the center of a national effort to improve educational performance through an agenda of explicit student learning standards, assessments of learning outcomes, and institutional accountability for performance. An additional $10 billion in federal funding for elementary and secondary education is proposed to accompany the stronger federal role (U.S. Office of Management and the Budget, 2003). So far, the strengthened federal policy role has been largely confined to K–12 education, although it could and, some argue, should be extended to higher education. As an example, the Bush Administration and Senator Joseph Lieberman have separately indicated a concern that the problems of low graduation rates and long time to degree should be addressed through the Higher Education Act. Thus, the law could evolve into a platform for a much-expanded federal presence in higher education. Should that occur, the federal definition of the credit hour as a time- and location-based measure of student learning will be at the center of a national debate about the future direction of higher education.

Higher Education Act

The central platform articulating the federal role in higher education is the Higher Education Act (see Exhibit 6.1), first enacted in 1965 as part of the Great Society legislation of the Johnson Administration. The Higher

Exhibit 6.1. Titles in the Higher Education Act

Title I.	General Provisions (definitions of terms used in the law)
Title II.	Teacher Quality Enhancement Grants for States and Partnerships
Title III.	Institutional Aid (Aid to Strengthen Institutions; Funds for Historically Black Colleges and Universities; Minority Science and Engineering Improvement Programs)
Title IV.	Student Aid (Pell grants; Early Outreach and Student Services Programs; Campus-based Aid; federal loans; State Partnership grant programs; analysis of student financial need; Robert Byrd scholarships; program, student, and institutional requirements for aid eligibility; program integrity for aid, including regulation of accreditation)
Title V.	Aid to Hispanic Serving Institutions
Title VI.	International Education Programs
Title VII.	Graduate and Postsecondary Education Programs

Source: U.S. Department of Education. Compilation of Federal Education Laws, Vol. 3: Higher Education. Washington, D.C.: U.S. Government Printing Office, 1999.

Education Act provides the statutory authorization for the federal student aid and other higher educational programs. These programs extend the model of the GI Bill because they are designed to provide federal funding to students rather than to institutions through vouchers that allow low-income students to attend college. Unlike the GI Bill, which was an entitlement granted on the basis of prior service, eligibility for federal student aid is largely determined by student economic need measured by a combination of income and the cost of education. The logic of the act is that student aid provides an ideal vehicle for promoting the dual federal roles of economic opportunity and excellence through grants aimed at the neediest students—grants that can be spent at any accredited college or university in the country (Gladieux and Wolanin, 1976). By allowing student enrollment choice to determine the flow of federal funds, the law enhances competition in higher education, thus (theoretically, at least) promoting institutional diversity through competition and enhancing quality. The portability of the student aid programs has been central to the transition of higher education from being institutionally determined and curriculum defined to a system that is increasingly student determined, through "portfolios" of programs built on sequences of courses taken at multiple institutions.

Federal Uses and Enforcement of the Credit Hour

The federal government uses the credit hour in several ways: as a measure of time on task and student progress to a degree; as a standard measure for reporting purposes, such as full-time-equivalent measures in enrollment reporting; and as a regulatory tool to enforce standards of time as a surrogate for quality. The credit hour is not the only vehicle that accomplishes these purposes, but it is built into a series of time-based measures that weave throughout the Higher Education Act. These involve provisions that affect academic calendars; time-to-degree measures; measure of educational costs; definitions of degree and enrollment levels; and definitions of campuses, branch campuses, and sites. In addition, the credit hour is embedded in many of the federal reporting requirements for institutions seeking to obtain student aid eligibility.

Many of these provisions have been put into the law to ensure program and financial integrity in the aid programs—that is, to prevent "diploma mills" and other perpetrators of financial fraud from participating in federal aid programs. Before 1992, federal standards for academic calendars and program length were not in statute. However, incidences of fraud and abuse in the aid programs (including several well-publicized closures of regionally accredited institutions) sent the student loan default rate to its highest levels ever. In 1992, Congress reacted by reauthorizing the law with provisions designed to strengthen both administrative and financial controls and improve quality control. Initially, it instituted the short-lived State Postsecondary Review Entity program, designed to partner the federal government with the states in a program to review institutions showing signs of institutional instability through high default rates, unstable finances, or poor pass rates of graduates on mandatory examinations. This program was clumsily implemented and became political dynamite within the higher education establishment, which led to its repeal.

However, the other measures instituted in the 1992 amendments that were aimed at fraud and abuse in the loan programs remain. These include a strengthened federal regulatory control over accreditation and federal administrative, reporting, and financial requirements designed to screen out marginal institutions. Many of these use time-based measures, such as academic calendars and program length, which are clearly designed as proxies for institutional quality, insofar as it is reflected in time on task. The 1992 law appears to have been successful in reducing student loan default (along with enrollments in for-profit institutions). At the same time, the reforms of the 1992 amendments have become problematic for many conventional institutions seeking to provide students with flexible enrollment options through alternative calendars (such as intensive short-course programs offered over two or three months) and distance learning. The problem of federal regulation of time-based measures was mentioned as an obstacle by several of the institutions reviewed in the companion chapter (Chapter Three) from this project on instructional innovation. These time-based measures are particularly difficult for institutions that serve a high number of part-time, older students through distance learning. Congress, however, has been loath to remove these requirements out of concern that to do so will again give rise to fraud in the student aid programs. In the 1998 reauthorization of the law, a "distance learning demonstration program" was designed to identify alternatives to time-based measures that nonetheless maintain integrity in the aid programs. This program is described in more detail later in this chapter.

Specific provisions that use the credit hour in some part of federal law are described below.

Institutional Eligibility. An institution must meet three conditions to be eligible to participate in the federal Title IV programs. It must be accredited by a federally recognized accreditor, licensed by the state in which it is located, and meet federal financial and administrative requirements for aid. The federal requirements for institutional eligibility also sometimes reach beyond the institution as a frame of reference for programs within institutions, in addition to student enrollment status. Institutional and programmatic requirements often weave back and forth with one another, creating confusion for the USDE as well as for institutions.

Definition of an Institution. The credit hour is embedded in the legal definition of an institution of higher education because the measure is built into degree requirements. An institution of higher education must award bachelor's degrees or two-year programs transferable to bachelor's-degree programs. Degree-granting programs are required by law to record course work in *credit hours,* defined as "A unit of measure representing an hour (50 minutes) of instruction over a 15-week period in a semester or trimester system or a 10-week period in a quarter system. It is applied toward the total number of hours needed for completing the requirements of a degree, diploma, certificate, or other formal award" (U.S. Department of Education, 2002, p. 4). Postsecondary or non-degree-granting institutions must record course work in *clock hours,* which are defined as a "unit of measure that represents an hour of scheduled instruction given to students; also referred to as a contact hour" (U.S. Department of Education, 2002, p. 4). It is important to note that the law references the credit hour only as a measure of time on task and a building block toward a degree. It is used synonymously with contact hours, implying that time spent outside of the classroom with no instructor physically present is not recognized for credit. The credit- and clock-hour requirements are built, in turn, into definitions of different degrees, diplomas, and instructional levels. However, the terms are not defined either in law or regulation, although they appear in an Integrated Postsecondary Education Data Surveys (IPEDS) data glossary (U.S. Department of Education, 2002).

Academic Year and Full-Time Enrollment. Institutions are required to offer at least thirty weeks of regularly scheduled instruction per year, during which "full-time undergraduate" students are expected to complete at least either twenty-four semester hours, thirty-six quarter hours, or nine hundred clock hours (20 U.S.C., Section 481).

Student Enrollment Status. In addition to demonstrating financial need for need-based aid programs, students must maintain the appropriate enrollment status to be eligible for financial aid. Students must be enrolled at least half-time (defined as more than six hours per week in semester hours) to be eligible for student loan aid (20 U.S.C. 1091, Section 484). Students may be eligible for grants if enrolled for less than twelve hours (considered "full-time" in semester hours), but the grant level is prorated based on the number of units of enrollment. The credit hour thus is used to establish the award levels for students with financial need (20 U.S.C. 1070a, Section 401). In the student loan program, borrowing limits are determined based on enrollment levels, with lower limits for lower-division than upper-division students and the highest limits for graduate and professional students (20 U.S.C. 1087dd, Section 464). To measure these award levels, the law determines student enrollment levels based on credits attained. Students enrolled as correspondence school students are precluded by regulation from being considered full-time students (34 C.F.R. 668.2, Section 668.2).

Fifty Percent Limits for Institutions and Programs. Institutions are not eligible for Title IV funding if more than 50 percent of their courses are offered through correspondence or telecommunications. The 50 percent limit is also extended to program eligibility within otherwise eligible institutions; for example, if more than 50 percent of the courses in a particular program are offered through telecommunications or correspondence, students enrolled in that program are not eligible for Title IV funding (20 U.S.C. 1001, Section 102 [a][3]). Nondegree programs are also required to offer courses for at least fifteen weeks, six hundred clock hours, sixteen semester hours, or twenty-four quarter hours (20 U.S.C. 1088, Section 481).

Satisfactory Academic Progress. The law also requires students to be continually enrolled and to maintain *satisfactory academic progress* (defined in the law as maintaining a C average) in order to retain student aid funding. This provision makes it difficult for institutions that enroll a high proportion of students taking only one or two courses to participate in the aid programs. The problems experienced by the University of Phoenix with the USDE, described in Chapter Three, are testament to consequences of this provision (20 U.S.C. 1091, Section 485 [C]).

Student Costs of Instruction. Award levels to needy students are based on educational costs, including tuition, fees, and for students attending more than half-time, living costs. Credit hours are used to compute tuition and fee costs for students enrolled less than full-time. They are also used to determine which students are eligible to receive grant funds for living and other expenses.

Enrollment Status, Graduation, and Defaults. Students are "continuously enrolled" based on whether they are registered as students from one term to the next, according to law. Determination of enrollment status is used to calculate attrition rates, measure satisfactory academic progress, and impose requirements for tuition refunds. Enrollment status also determines when students who have loans enter their "payback" periods. Students who move from full- to less than half-time status become ineligible to participate in the loan programs (20 U.S.C. 1087dd, Section 464).

Disbursement. Time-based measures are used to determine the sequence for disbursing loan and grant funds to institutions. Institutions with either nonstandard academic calendars must negotiate payment periods for disbursement of aid with the USDE (U.S. Department of Education, 2002).

Regulation of Accreditors. Institutions must be accredited by an agency recognized by the USDE secretary as a "reliable authority as to the quality of education or training offered" (20 U.S.C. 1099B [a], Section 496). The federal government has relied on accrediting agencies to certify institutional quality since the time of the GI Bill. Accreditation, a system of peer review that uses commonly agreed-to standards of criteria for quality, has been around since the late 1800s. Accreditation historically has been self-regulated through an internal "recognition" process managed by the Council for Postsecondary Accreditation and its successor agency, the Council for Higher Education Accreditation. However, as the problems in the aid programs began to accumulate, the federal government increasingly incorporated the previously voluntary tools of self-regulation into federal regulation and ultimately into statute. The 1992 amendments represent the most aggressive expansion of federal regulation to date. The Higher Education Act of 1965 articulates criteria that agencies must meet to be federally recognized, stating "[it] consistently applies and enforces standards that ensure that the courses or program of instruction, training or study offered by the institution of higher education, including distance education courses or programs, are of sufficient quality to achieve, for the duration of the accreditation period, the stated objective for which the courses or programs are offered" (U.S. Department of Education, 1999, p. 496). The types of standards that must be in place for an accreditor to apply for recognition are outlined in the law. These minimum standards are:

- Success with respect to student achievement in relation to the institution's mission
- Curricula
- Faculty
- Facilities, equipment, and supplies
- Fiscal and administrative capacity as appropriate to the specified scale of operations
- Student support services
- Recruiting and admissions practices, academic calendars, catalogues, publications, grading, and advertising
- Measures of program length and the objectives of the degrees or credentials offered
- Record of student complaints received by or available to the agency
- Record of compliance with Title IV responsibilities (20 U.S.C. 1099b, [a][4] and [5])

As the discussion in Chapter Five shows, there are wide variations among the different accreditation agencies in their enforcement of the credit hour. Whereas accreditors and the federal government have a dual role in external enforcement of the credit hour, clearly accreditors generally view the measure as a flexible device for recording student course work, whereas the federal government seems to view it as a hard measure of time on task, related to student learning.

Institutional Reporting Requirements

The USDE has a significant role in data collection and information dissemination in addition to its program administration and regulatory responsibilities. It does this through periodic surveys of institutions. Some of these surveys are based on samples of institutions or students; others are required of all institutions that participate in Title IV. All institutions are required to report on institutional finance, staffing, and student enrollments in a series of surveys collectively known as the IPEDS. One of the IPEDS requires institutions to report on student credit-hour activity; the rest of the surveys embed the credit hour in measures of full- and part-time enrollment status. The IPEDS dictionary is the one place where the federal government provides specific definitions for the credit hour and many of the other time-based measures that are extensions of it. These reporting requirements by themselves, therefore, perpetuate the most literal interpretations of the credit unit.

The USDE also requires institutions to provide consumer information about their performance in the "Student Right to Know" report. The Student Right to Know law requires institutions to provide the public with information about costs, student aid, program availability, and graduation rates. The graduation rate requirement in the Student Right to Know law requires institutions to document cohort progress of entering students for five years from first full-time freshmen enrollment, with credit-hour accumulation as the measure of academic progress. The nature of the Student Right to Know law allows some variation among institutions in the method they may use to report on attrition and graduation rates. The Student Right to Know time-based performance statistics have become the standard measure for reporting on institutional "productivity" for degree production, a measure that is increasingly being used in reporting formats of state accountability.

Distance Education Demonstration Project

As a result of growing interest in promoting distance education, Congress established a Distance Education Demonstration Project in the 1998 reauthorization of the Higher Education Act. The law states that the purpose of the project was to test the quality and viability of expanded distance-education programs, determine the most effective means of delivering quality education through distance learning, and determine the "appropriate level of federal assistance to students enrolled in distance learning programs" (20 U.S.C. 1092, Section 486). The law invited applications from as many as fifteen distance-education institutions or programs not otherwise eligible to participate in the aid program. The following institutions applied and sought waivers for specific provisions:

Capella University, Minneapolis, Minnesota: sought waivers on the 50 percent rules and the length of the academic year

Community Colleges of Colorado (fourteen institutions): sought waivers on 50 percent rules, length of academic year, week of instructional time, and satisfactory academic progress

Connecticut Distance Learning Consortium (twenty-five institutions): sought waivers on 50 percent rules, length of academic year, and week of instructional time

Florida State University, Tallahassee: sought waivers on 50 percent rules

Franklin University, Columbus, Ohio: sought waivers on 50 percent rules

LDS Church Education System (four institutions): sought waivers on 50 percent rules, academic year, week of instruction, and full-time students

New York University, New York: sought waivers on 50 percent rules, academic year, and week of instruction

North Dakota University system (eleven institutions): sought waivers on 50 percent rules, academic year, week of instruction, and full-time students

Quest Education Corporation-Kaplan College: sought waivers on 50 percent rules, academic year, and week of instruction

Southern Christian University, Montgomery, Alabama: sought waivers on 50 percent rules

Texas Tech University, Lubbock: sought waivers on 50 percent rules, academic year, week of instruction, and full-time students

University of Maryland-University College, College Park: sought waivers on 50 percent rules, academic year, and full-time students

Western Governors' University (WGU): WGU was specifically mentioned in the authorizing statute (U.S. Department of Education, 2002)

A first year's progress report on the Distance Education Demonstration Project was submitted to Congress in January 2001. In that report, the USDE discusses a possible "student-based" student aid delivery model as an alternative to the institutionally based model. WGU is used as the institution to model the possibilities of a "student-based delivery model," with features such as

Individual start dates

Establishing time periods within which full-time students would be expected to complete a degree or certificate to be used as the basis for determining student enrollment status to determine award levels

Definition of the academic year as 365 days long

Awards based on estimated cost of attendance

Division of academic year into two equal payment periods

Adding courses during the payment period

Multiple disbursements within payment periods to accommodate disbursement of funds as costs are incurred

Ongoing monitoring of academic progress, as measured by completion of competency examinations or components of competency examinations

Special Report on the "Twelve-Hour Rule"

Although the law contains the "thirty-week" rule, it does not define what an academic week is, something done by regulation through the USDE in the twelve-hour and thirty-week rule. This regulation came to be a lightning rod for debates about distance learning. Because the rule was regulatory and not statutory, in 2001 Congress directed the USDE to renegotiate the rules with affected parties through a process known as "negotiated rule making." In July 2001, the USDE issued a special report on the twelve-hour rule, much of which dwelt on the question of comparability of quality for distance-delivered courses and whether credits can be uncoupled from measures of time. The issue became contentious within the higher education community in Washington, D.C., with the American Association of University Professors and the American Federation of Teachers leading the charge to maintain the twelve-hour rule as a way of stemming the growth of distance-based learning. They lost the fight, and the twelve-hour regulation was abandoned by the USDE in 2002.

Summary and Conclusions

The federal government, through the USDE, has multiple roles with regard to the credit-hour measure: as a measure of class time, a surrogate for progress to a degree, a means of standardizing activities into common measures (full-time enrollments, instructional costs, and student progress to degree), a data-reporting element, the core unit of instructional time, and a surrogate for quality. Because the measure is required to be reported by all institutions as a condition of federal funding, the federal government—more than any other single entity—perpetuates the enforcement of the credit hour as a time-based measure.

The federal government used the credit hour first as a measure of activity and a reporting standard but has incrementally increased its use as a means of enforcing administrative and financial integrity in the student aid program. Because the federal government does not recognize any alternatives to the credit hour as valid surrogates for instructional time, its enforcement of the credit hour through standard academic calendars and instructional delivery constructs poses difficulties for institutions wanting to offer instruction through alternative calendars and teaching modalities. These issues led to the creation of the federal demonstration programs to test alternatives to time-based measures and to debates about the now defunct twelve-hour rule. These are topics that have come to be politically symbolic as an imagined dividing line between an institutionally based and faculty-centered higher education system and a system that is defined primarily in terms of individual courses and the accumulation of student credits. The credit hour and its preservation, change, or dissolution thus are at the center of a larger national debate about the meaning of higher education and the means of its delivery.

References

Gladieux, L. E., and Wolanin, T. R. *Congress and the Colleges.* San Francisco: New Lexington Press, 1976.

National Commission on Excellence in Education. *A Nation at Risk.* Washington, D.C.: U.S. Government Printing Office, 1983.

U.S. Department of Education. *Compilation of Federal Education Laws, Vol. 3: Higher Education.* Washington, D.C.: U.S. Government Printing Office, 1999.

U.S. Department of Education. *Instructions for the Integrated Postsecondary Education Data Surveys.* Washington, D.C.: U.S. Government Printing Office, 2002.

U.S. Office of Management and the Budget. *Federal Budget for Fiscal 2003.* [http://w3access.gpo.gov/usbudget/fy2003/pdf/hist.pdf]. Washington, D.C.: U.S. Government Printing Office, 2003.

JANE V. WELLMAN is a senior associate with the Institute for Higher Education Policy in Washington, D.C.

7

One of the most pervasive uses of the credit hour is as a workload and resource measure in public budgeting, although it is often a poor proxy for measuring workload and resource use. It works to the particular disadvantage of public community colleges.

The Credit Hour and Public Budgeting

Jane V. Wellman

This chapter discusses the ways the credit hour has come to be used by public funding systems in higher education. Research for this analysis consisted of reviewing published literature on state budgeting for higher education and interviewing national experts on public budgeting. Confined to a review of the credit hour in public operating budgets, the review does not go into the ways that the credit hour is used as a budgeting tool in private institutions, nor does it explore the other types of budgets in higher education (capital outlay, auxiliary enterprise, hospitals, and restricted-fund budgeting). However, the credit hour and its derivatives are used in enrollment-driven budgets, which are common in private and public institutions and factor into capital budgeting as well. Aspects of the analysis may generalize well beyond public operating budgets. The analysis also is largely confined to a review of the way that funds are distributed as part of the budget process, as distinct from the larger topic of public finance, which touches upon revenues and subsidy policies and not just the ways that funds are distributed.

Changing Funding Climate

The topic of state financing for public higher education is under discussion in virtually every state at the beginning of 2003. Following many good funding years in the last half of the 1990s, the combination of tax cuts and the 2002 recession have created the worst year for state budgets since the end of World War II. The current shortfalls are revealing deep fault lines created by structural imbalances between revenues and expenditures in most states, which means that even when the current crisis is over, the long-term funding trajectory for higher education remains bleak. This is because higher education is funded as part of the discretionary budget at the state level, and discretionary programs have been declining as a percentage of total state spending for the past decade because of revenue shortfalls and mandatory spending increases in entitlement programs such as health care.

In the absence of comprehensive state budget reform, both on the revenue and expenditure side, higher education funding will likely continue to erode as a percentage of state spending. These shortfalls are occurring at a time when many states are experiencing unprecedented enrollment demand for higher education. Institutions have instituted sharp increases in tuition to help make up the gap, although the revenue from tuitions has not fully replaced lost state revenues. The combination of enrollment increases and revenue shortfalls has created a double whammy for most institutions, who must find ways to add room for new students on a declining revenue base. They have also led to a heightened interest in new ways to rationalize funding for higher education. In this climate, the role of the credit hour in state budgeting deserves heightened attention, either as a hindrance or a potential tool, in the needed restructuring of finance for higher education.

General Approaches to Public Budgeting

As the history of the credit hour described in Chapter One shows, one of the design purposes for it behind the early work of The Carnegie Foundation for the Advancement of Teaching (cited in Chapter One) was to create an activity measure that could be used to normalize costs and compare production costs across institutions. So it is not surprising that the credit hour has evolved into one of the most important elements for public budgeting, both as a building block for student enrollments and as an analytic tool for assessing how resources are used, through cost measurement and analysis of student flow.

The term *public budgeting* encompasses a complex political process within which public institutions request and receive funds from the state and, in turn, distribute the resources to campuses and departments. The overarching policy goal for a public budgeting system is to ensure that the state is meeting its obligations to support the state's mission for the institutions in a way that is credible, serves the purpose of framing a public discussion about purposes and contributions, can be part of a system of accountability (audits, performance reports), and provides a level of resources that is adequate to the mission of the institution. The technical aspects of budgeting work in tandem with the political and governmental actors in a state to determine the basis for distributing resources.

It is axiomatic in higher education that the budget is the most powerful public policy tool for influencing institutional behavior because people naturally react to the positive and negative incentives built into any system for distributing funds. As a result, states and institutions use the public budgeting process to articulate policy goals for higher education in terms that have currency within the political budget process. This is done through plans, performance measures, formulas, and negotiated agreements.

The budget process typically is a multiyear, multistage process, moving from planning to budget request and approval, appropriation, and audit or evaluation. There are two basic areas in which the budget process operates: between the university and the state and within universities or colleges. Understanding the role that the credit-hour measure plays in all of these stages is of interest, but much of the discussion will focus on its role as a tool for public resource allocation and accountability. The primary focus is on the credit hour and the budget relation between the state and the university.

All public colleges and universities organize their operating budgets into broad program categories to distinguish between different types of institutional activities. These categories were initially developed in the 1960s and 1970s on a voluntary basis, led by the work of Dennis Jones and his colleagues at the National Center for Higher Education Management Systems. Over time, the terminology has become standardized, and it now is embedded in federal Integrated Postsecondary Education Data Surveys (IPEDS) and state reporting formats (see Chapter Six for a more complete description of IPEDS). The categories are used for budgeting and planning and for reporting expenditures. The broad categories and the types of activities are budgetary and expenditures detailed in Table 7.1 (see the IPEDS "data dictionary" for a complete list of program categories and guidelines to institutions on criteria for assigning functions to them, U.S. Department of Education, 2002).

Table 7.1. Higher Education Budget Expenditures and Activities

Budget or Expenditure Category	General Activities
Instruction	General instruction, departmental administration, and departmental research
Research	Organized research (typically externally funded)
Public service	Organized activities such as community schools, public cultural events
Academic support	Libraries and museums, computing services
Student services	Counseling, advising, financial aid administration, student health services, academic tutoring, and job placement
Institutional support	Central institutional administrative services such as admissions, accounting, executive management, planning, and institutional research
Plant operation or maintenance	Building and grounds maintenance
Scholarships and fellowships	Student financial aid grants and loans
Auxiliary enterprises	Self-supporting activities such as dormitories, cafeterias, and bookstores
Hospitals and clinics	Self-supporting (or partially self-supporting) hospitals and clinics

These categories are only proxies for the behaviors associated with them. There is a blurring between instruction and research, particularly at the graduate level but also in terms of faculty time. As an example, unfunded departmental research is recorded as an instructional activity in most institutions, whereas extramurally funded research or organized research (organized into institutes or centers that are administratively separate from academic departments) is labeled "Research." Most department-level administration is categorized as an instructional expenditure, whereas central administrative services are called "institutional support." The guidelines for distributing costs across multiple functions have become regularized over the years through the work of the National Center for Higher Education Management Systems (NCHEMS) and the voluntary activities of the National Association of College and University Business Officers and are now codified in IPEDS and other reporting protocols (Jenny, 1996). Nonetheless, institutions have some flexibility in deciding how to categorize expenditures, which can make comparisons of costs at the program level between institutions imprecise.

Evolution of Different Approaches to Budgeting

The history of how the credit hour became a building block in budgeting for public colleges and universities throughout the country in the 1960s has been documented by several states—California, Texas, Illinois, Michigan, New York, and Wisconsin. There are common themes among them, although the specifics differ. The states' different histories reflect the diverse organization and governance of higher education and whether there are multicampus "system" boards or statewide governing boards. Understanding these internal and external political dynamics helps to reveal the technical aspects of the budgeting systems that developed from them (Jones, 1984; Lasher and Greene, 2001; Douglass, 2000).

In the 1960s, as many state universities began to expand from single campuses to multicampus systems, developing appropriate budget procedures became one of the first priorities for new multicampus statewide systems. (These were sometimes segmental-level governing boards in states like New York, Wisconsin, Florida, and California with those governance structures or state-level boards in states like Ohio, Texas, and Virginia that did not have system boards). The boards had to figure out how to balance the different needs of internal institutional constituencies with the broader state interest. The internal institutional tensions were particularly acute between the research universities and the comprehensive colleges and between established and growing institutions. The external constituencies needed to know that funding requests were based on real needs and that resources were subsequently used for the purposes for which they were requested. The state also wanted a way to compare funding requests across systems or institutions to confirm that the criteria for funding them were reasonably equitable. In sum, systems were needed that allowed budget decisions to be based on transparent public information and that used ground rules for comparing funding needs that were perceived as equitable among the different players. To allow for the development of consensus on priorities, they also needed systems to be based on previously developed, publicly vetted plans.

The basic model that emerged in all states was a cost-based, incremental budgeting system. In these systems, annual funding requests are developed and resources allocated based on the prior year's use of resources, with adjustments based on workload and program needs. The basic formula for determining unit costs per credit hour was developed by analyzing patterns of past resource use within institutions, sometimes with additions for program improvement or to achieve internal funding equities. Credit-hour costs could also be used to predict future resource requirements, through models such as the Resource Requirement Prediction Models developed by NCHEMS. To the question of which came first, the credit-hour measure or the money, the answer is the money: the credit-hour formulas were created to help document how existing base resources were being spent. Similar unit-costs systems could be used across institutions with different missions through the assignment of weights to reflect the different missions, program, or discipline mixes associated with different funding levels. For instance, if a flagship research campus spent more money per full-time equivalent (FTE) than a comprehensive campus, the higher funding levels would be built into the weights used to frame the formulas per FTE. Once the formulas were developed, they then perpetuated the prior expenditure patterns.

The credit hour and FTE became the default tool for measuring costs not only for instruction but also for areas such as academic and institutional support, largely because there were agreements about how to measure activity in these areas. The core cost measure that drove all budgets was an average cost per FTE student enrollment, with the credit hour as the basic unit for measuring cost per student (Bowen, 1980; Jenny, 1996).

In many states—California, New York, Indiana, Minnesota, and New Jersey, for instance—the early budget systems were confined to public four-year institutions and excluded community colleges. Community colleges were funded as part of county government, and those budget systems were based on K–12 funding models. The budget models for community colleges in these states, as a result, looked much more like extensions of K–12 apportionment formulas, which sometimes measured funds per average daily attendance rather than FTE. Unlike higher education, K–12 and community colleges originally did not report budgets or expenditures in the program areas (described previously); funds were simply apportioned based on average daily attendance. Their enrollment measures are generated in much the same way as FTE, through collections of earned student credits. A key difference between higher education and K–12 is that K–12 graduation requirements are typically defined (and regulated) in terms of course requirements that are translated into Carnegie units (see Chapter One), whereas degree requirements in public higher education are generally defined by credits rather than courses. (This issue is explored in greater depth in Chapter Six). Also, the student credit-unit measures in K–12 and the community colleges are based on "positive time recording" of attendance, following mandatory attendance laws. In contrast, the criteria for determining how the credit hour and FTE are assigned in the four-year sectors are largely determined at the institutional or departmental level, with no external audit to ensure consistency.

Although rough parallels exist between the community colleges and the four-year institutions in many subsequent budget developments, the roots of the community college funding models in K–12 mean that the layer of control over the basic measure of work for these institutions is more restrictive and that the state has a different role in both governing and paying for the enterprise.

Paralleling the growth in budgeting systems was the development of more sophisticated management information systems, which required data reporting from campuses on workload measures, including campus-based credit hours, by level of instruction and discipline and mode of instruction (lecture, seminar, laboratory, or discussion). The more sophisticated data allowed refinements in cost estimates, which in turn fed changes in budget systems. This led to increasingly sophisticated budget formulas, moving from average cost per FTE across all functions to ones that differentiated costs within institutions at the discipline level, level of instruction, or departmental level.

A prototype of an early state budget formula can be found in Dennis Jones' (1984) book, *Higher Education Budgeting at the State Level,* taken from Kentucky (see Table 7.2). The credit hour is the basic building block for the primary mission areas (instruction and academic support), and most of the other areas are calculated as a percentage of the core budget. Student services is the one major area with workload formulas that are not driven by the credit hour, being based instead on head-count enrollments.

Jones also provides examples from other states—Missouri, Indiana, and Wisconsin—that show various approaches to differentiating between fixed, variable, and marginal costs in the different formulas.

Over the years, there have been numerous experiments with techniques for measuring costs and rationalizing budgets for noninstructional areas. An interesting example of one comes from an effort to develop funding standards for the care and storage of laboratory animals, an area clearly only tangentially related to the credit hour. The following quotation is taken from an internal memorandum in the Office of the President of the University of California in the 1970s, which proposed a basis for measuring workload for storing laboratory animals (internal memorandum, names deleted for obvious reasons; the proposal was never adopted).

Table 7.2. An Early State Budget Formula

Program Area	Guideline	Comments
Primary mission areas: includes support for regular session and summer school instruction, plus academic support and funding to allow institutions to carry out their missions	Number of credit hours by level and discipline times cost per credit-hour rates plus adjustments for instruction by institutional type based on peer institutions	A typical base-plus-rate approach coupled with a percentage of base factor; the credit-hour figures are 3-year averages to buffer enrollment shifts; rates per credit hour are determined on peer institution basis
Kentucky residency program	Number of hours staff times FTE faculty per hours staff times average compensation plus academic support and departmental operating expenses	A different approach from that above, based on salary rates, emphasizing student-faculty ratios, and using credit hour as driver for both
Area health education system	Number of student weeks times rate per week	Straight base plus calculation
Preparatory (remedial) education	Number of freshmen and sophomores scoring less than 12 on American College Test at cost per student	Straight base plus calculation
Libraries, museums, and galleries	Base plus number of credit hours in excess of 50,000 times cost per credit hour (different factors applied to community colleges)	Fixed plus variable cost calculation
Student services	Base plus head-count enrollment times rate per head-count enrollment	Fixed plus variable calculation
Maintenance and operation of physical plant	Square feet and rate per square feet plus utilized acres times rate per acre plus rental and lease amounts minus indirect cost recovery	Combination of rate plus base, categorical and contract funding
Organized research	Percentage times sponsored research plus mandated programs	Percentage of base factor coupled with categorical programs for institutes, centers, etc.
Community service	Base plus base for specific missions plus mandated programs	Fixed base for maintenance of capacity plus categorical programs
Institutional support	Percentage of all previous components except for hospitals	Percentage of base calculation
Scholarships and fellowships	Percentage of tuition revenues plus state matching funds required for federal programs	Rate plus base

Source: Jones (1984, pp. 98–100). Reprinted with permission.

Studies of animal cost data of various institutions throughout the nation and of the economically managed colonies in Naval Biological Laboratory and Cancer Research Genetic Laboratory, indicate that the laboratory mouse fulfills the . . . prerequisites to serve as a unit for the measurement of workload. Accordingly the *mouse equivalent unit* (MEU) has been created and can be used to estimate the space, cost and personnel needs for the housing and care of any experimental animal species. This unit can also serve as a base for computing recharges to departments using animals in a central Vivarium. Mouse equivalent units for several species are shown in the table below:

Species	Mouse Equivalent Units*
Mouse	1
Rat	4
Hamster	3
Guinea Pig	5
Rabbit	16
Cat	32
Dog	50
Chicken	10
Pigeon	4
Small birds	2

*Applicable only to caged animals

One mouse equivalent unit requires 0.125 square feet of space and 0.0004167 FTE staff. Total cost of maintaining one MEU ranges from 1 to 1.5 cents per day depending on the efficiency of the physical facilities, labor costs, etc., and on the fiscal and management policies.

One FTE is needed for each 2,400 MEUs and includes:

FTE	
Animal technicians and caretakers	0.6
Senior animal technicians	0.12
Principal animal technicians	0.03
Weekend caretakers	0.1
Cage washing and storage attendants	0.075
Clinical personnel	0.075

The unit recharge cost of the MEU includes:

Labor	55–60%
Feed and bedding	20–25%
Caging & other supplies	12–20%
Maintenance	3–5%

For prospective workload and budget estimates the number of square feet of animal space available must be used as the base figure, since census and species of animals to be housed are not known. As animal census stabilizes, the actual number of animals maintained can be used as a base and budgets can be refined.

Jones (1984) and Lasher and Greene (2001) have commented on the tendency for states and institutions to refine and change budgets over time. Each budget system has certain advantages and some disadvantages that then give rise to the next generation of improvements. In fact, some of the reform efforts were developed to compensate for the perceived deficiencies of incremental and formula-based funding, which were that they perpetuate the status quo and reward institutions for spending money rather than for setting priorities and accomplishing results.

One of the early reforms was a variation on formula budgeting known as program-planning budgeting systems (PPBS). The PPBS and successive generations of similar techniques were designed to strengthen the relationships between institutional planning, state policy, and funding. They typically maintained the formula for generating the base budget and then added resources for new initiatives based on previously developed and agreed-on plans. The PPBS came into use in the mid- to late 1970s, around the time that higher education enrollments began to level off or (in some states) to decline. Because the systems were designed to provide new money for planned growth, they tended to fall into disuse, to be replaced by old base-plus systems and formulas. Some public policy analysts also began to criticize the basic techniques for building cost-based budgets as excessively technical, making them impenetrable to all but insiders in the budget process. Aaron Wildavsky was one of the earliest and most eloquent critics of formula budgeting. In his 1998 classic treatise, *The Politics of the Budget Process*, he says that the goal of a public budget system should be to frame policy issues in a way that engages rather than avoids debate—better for the public interest than technical formulas that insulate institutions from political decision making and increase disagreement about the basis for distributing resources. According to Wildavsky, PPBS were "no PP, all BS" (testimony from Wildavsky to the California Joint Legislative Budget Committee, early 1980s).

The 1980s and early 1990s were times of retrenchment, and institutions and states that had not already done so began to throw out formula budgets in favor of base plus-minus budgeting. One of the reasons for the change was that many institutions had stable or declining enrollments, and the incentive to document workload needs for new growth had been replaced with a desire to hold onto base budgets. Budget justifications continued to be submitted at a technical level to departments of finance, showing detailed enrollments and credit-hour data, but these were primarily used for internal allocation of resources rather than external justification of them.

The next generation of budget reform took hold in the 1990s, at a time of a shift in the nature of state funding for higher education and a new level of attention to public accountability. In almost all states, structural budget gaps between current fund revenues and expenditures began to be revealed, gaps that were exacerbated by the recession of the early 1990s (Hovey, 2000). Higher education is funded as a discretionary item, which means that in times of retrenchment, it disproportionately loses state revenue. Historic commitments to formula budgets were set aside or abandoned as states reduced operating budget support for higher education. Institutions were forced to cut budgets and increase tuitions. Over the decade of the 1990s, the percentage of education and general revenues from state and local sources to higher education declined in all sectors—by 8 percent in public research universities, 11 percent in public four-year institutions, and 8 percent in community colleges (National Center for Education Statistics, 2002). Nationwide, at the end of the decade, the balance of funding responsibility had fundamentally changed in public higher education, with state funds making up less than half of total revenues for the four-year-sector higher education and remaining just over a half in the public two-year sector. As states tightened their purse strings, institutions successfully negotiated reformulations of budget control practices, shifting away from funding formula accompanied by line-item budget control toward block budgets augmented and based on negotiated performance agreements. Budgets were still distributed largely on a base plus-minus basis, but the pretense of control over details of expenditures was largely abandoned in favor of negotiated agreements about goals and performance measures. In many states, the changes in budgeting were accompanied by changes in governance, away from state regulatory control over spending and greater institutional autonomy. This represented an important change from the days of cost-based funding because the performance goals that were used in most states were typically based on accountability measures for institutional performance rather than past patterns of resource use. However, as Burke and others have shown, the funds based on performance that were set aside to be distributed typically represented only a fraction of total state funds (Burke and Serban, 1998).

A look at the basis for documenting performance in several of the states with these funding systems shows that many of the performance measures continue to rely on credit-hour-generated measures: enrollment rates, persistence and time to degree, graduation rates, credits attempted, number of credits in remedial or noncredit instruction, and class size. (Ewell [1999] explores the types of data used in performance budgeting and the advantages and disadvantages of different measures for accomplishing different purposes.) However, unlike previous generations of budget formulas, these measures are not the sole basis for incentive funding. Other measures that are meant to be proxies for student learning and other dimensions of quality are also used: pass rates on licensure examinations, number of students going on to graduate school, average salaries earned by graduates, number of courses taught by regular faculty, and diversification of revenues are a few examples.

Ewell (1999) and others have commented that performance funding represents an extension of existing systems for formula budgeting in higher education. The base budget is rolled forward and new funds added for workload increases associated with enrollment growth and cost of living, after which incentive funds are added based on prior years' performance. In times of budget growth, these new revenues can be important levers for institutional behavior. In times of retrenchment, however, funds to maintain the baseplus workload and inflation come before performance funds. In the current climate, the game has shifted away from documenting the need for new resources to competition to hold onto the existing base. This means that the incentives for institutional change associated with new resources are weaker than those to maintain the status quo.

Advantages and Disadvantages of the Credit Hour in Relation to Public Budgeting

The credit hour has many advantages as a tool in budget development. Unlike many of the newer efforts to measure performance and document learning outcomes, the data systems that are used to document the credit hour H are well established and credible. The credit hour is widely recognized, and the customs for using it both to document activity and to standardize unit costs have gained wide acceptance. It is used in all institutions (even those that measure courses as single units can translate these into credit hours) and thus can be used to standardize measures and compare institutions on a reasonably even basis.

Credit-hour-based budget systems work under some circumstances better than others. They are particularly well suited for distributing instructional resources to mature—that is, not start-up—institutions in times of enrollment growth. However, when enrollments stagnate or decline, credit-hour budget systems create incentives for institutions to compete rather than to cooperate, because the incentive is always for growth. The credit hour's use as the building block for FTE creates various problems because of the limitations of FTE measures. FTE assumes a norm of a "full-time-equivalent" student, and the formulas used to generate base budgets reward full-time over part-time. The FTE norm may have been appropriate in the 1970s when the base budgets were built, but they are increasingly problematic as higher education has become a version of "Lake Woebegone," where the majority of students are "nontraditional," clearly calling into question regulatory and budget techniques that reward full-time as a preferred state of being (Choy, 2002).

The credit hour has most face validity as a translator of instructional workload, but it has less credibility as a measure of administrative, academic, or student support activity. Because instructional spending is less than half of total spending in all public higher education (nationally, expenditures for instruction are around 35 percent for research universities, 40 percent for comprehensive teaching institutions, and 43 percent for community colleges), this means that most of the "base" budget is justified primarily in relation to credit hours rather than other performance measures. There may be no getting around this basic fact for administrative and service areas: the somewhat absurd example of the "mouse equivalent unit" shows the limitations of workload measures outside of the instructional area.

The credit hour by its nature is best at measuring activity in credit-bearing instructional courses, particularly regularly scheduled lecture formats. It is less reliable as a measure of activity for noncredit instruction or for different types of "irregular" instruction—whether in graduate seminars, dissertation supervision, remedial education, or community-based learning. In this respect, it is a better tool for public budgeting for comprehensive institutions than for research universities or community colleges. When combined with the historic funding differences between these two sectors and the governance structures that are part of this history, the differences translate to systemic funding inequities for the community colleges:

The instructional mission of community colleges encompasses noncredit and credit activity. Noncredit activity ranges from remedial education, community education, and some vocational courses to adult education. Many state funding systems either do not fund noncredit activity or fund it at a unit-cost level different from credit-bearing activity.

Average-cost funding systems work better for institutions with a wide range of programs and instructional audiences because they can generate internal cross-subsidies to move revenues from low- to high-cost programs. This occurs in the four-year sectors through allocation away from low-cost disciplines like humanities and social sciences to laboratory sciences and performing arts. It also can occur through reallocation from lower-division to graduate-level courses. The community colleges have less freedom to generate internal cross-subsidies to pay for high- versus low-cost programs.

The basic construct of the credit hour, which presumes both out-of-class and in-class time, works better for academic than for vocational programs (see Chapters One and Five). Vocational programs typically are more classroom contact-hour dependent than degree programs, in which much of the activity occurs outside the classroom, so they will cost more than other types of programs. Community colleges pay for these types of programs by reducing faculty costs through hiring part-time or adjunct faculty.

The internal governance structure of community colleges, deriving in many states from their origins as part of the K–12 system, means that faculty have less explicit authority over academic policy than in four-year institutions. One of the consequences of this weaker role for faculty may be that the institutions are more regulated by external administrators than is true in four-year institutions. The results of the survey in Chapter Two certainly show that the public two-year institutions more often regulate the basis for awarding credit in relation to class time (see Chapter Two). This is probably because many community college regulatory and funding systems evolved from K–12 systems, and positive, time-based recording of workload was enforced. Although the audit capacity for these is eroded in most places, the habits remain. The basis for the unit is much more self-referential in the four-year institutions, where there is no regular internal institutional or external agency audit of the basis for assigning credits to classes.

Accountability and performance measures that measure persistence and time-to-degree measures can be a disadvantage for community colleges because so many of their students attend part-time, and many require academic remediation.

Funding problems in research universities are caused by the complexities of the joint products of research and instruction and the inability to isolate departmental research from instruction. Many of the activities of the research universities are not readily translatable to credit-hour designation. However, the research universities (unlike the community colleges or comprehensive institutions) more often have institutional autonomy to self-define the terms under which credit hours are assigned to activities. To recognize the higher costs of graduate education, they historically have assigned differential weights to credit hours generated in upper-division and graduate instruction to subsume departmental research and lower teaching loads into instructional costs. They also have developed norms for assigning credit hours to out-of-class work that are more commonly accepted than those of comprehensive or community colleges. In most institutions, dissertation-level doctoral students are assigned full-time status—receiving twelve credit hours—despite the fact that they no longer take regularly scheduled classes.

One of the biggest drawbacks to the credit-hour method for building budgets has to do with the incentive structures created within institutions. Faculty and administrators know (or believe they know) that they generate resources from the state for credit hours, without regard to learning outcomes, curriculum sequences, learning integrity, or often even the unit cost of instruction. This means that all incentives are to keep enrollments growing or—in the absence of enrollment demand—to generate credit hours. Funding incentives for institutions to pay attention to curriculum and to reduce low-enrollment courses are relatively weak because all credit hours "count" toward funding equally. Incentives for institutions to pay a lot of attention to instruction-related activities that do not generate credit hours are similarly weak. These types of service centers may be as or more important to students than course-driven credit-hour activities, particularly in an environment where most students are part-time and commute. The credit hour is not by itself the cause of the problem, but its role in the generation of resources perpetuates behaviors in which institutions always have an incentive to add instructional credits but not necessarily to look at whole modules of learning. The performance-driven budget measures were developed in large part to try to address the problem of internal incentive structures. However, because performance measures are often not funded or represent only a fraction of resources, the basic behavioral patterns remain unchanged.

Public Policy Question

Is the credit hour a problem for public policy in its role as a driver of public budgets? The answer is probably both yes and no. The activity measure is recognized and works reasonably well. There are no other readily agreed-on measures of workload, for instruction or other activities. The credit hour is embedded in regular assessments and audits and meets goals of transparency and comparability. The credit hour itself does not determine the level of funds associated with the unit of work; funding levels are determined based on the previous year's use of funds, institutional mission, state-funding capacity, and political negotiations. But once the level of funds has been established, the credit-hour-driven measures perpetuate existing patterns for distributing resources.

The credit hour itself is an imperfect measure of resource need for many aspects of the mission of higher education—parts of the instructional mission in the community colleges, the departmental research and graduate education mission in research universities, and noninstructional activity in all sectors. The measure is not externally validated in public four-year institutions, so it may not reflect comparable or equitable measures for assigning the credits to work. And it creates incentives in institutions for perpetual growth in credit hours, without regard to learning, degree attainment, or efficiency in production. Within institutions, as a result, it carries disincentives to attend to curriculum coherence, to cooperate among departments, or to focus energy on new measures of student learning, if only because they will receive the same level of resources without doing any of these things. New types of budgeting systems that go beyond credit-hour drivers overcome some of this, but the inequities are now built into the base.

The credit-hour measure is at one level irrelevant to the larger questions of state funding for higher education discussed at the outset of this chapter. The structural gaps that threaten discretionary state funding occur because of revenue and expenditure patterns affecting all state spending. These are not caused by the credit-hour measure and will not be solved by changing it. At the same time, the ongoing shortfalls in state funding are causing a fresh look at the allocation methods for higher education and are raising questions about the possible need to rethink historic funding patterns between the different sectors of higher education. The issues of equitable distribution of base resources are becoming increasingly important state policy issues. State policymakers and educators are just beginning to grapple with core questions of the role of state funding versus tuition revenues for research universities, comprehensive colleges, and community colleges. As they do so, the role of the credit hour as a primary determinant of the state revenue base will become increasingly prominent.

In summary, we sought answers to two questions in this exploration about the credit hour and budgets: whether its application has become a barrier to innovation in teaching and learning within institutions and whether its use in public budgeting creates any systemic inequities between institutions or sectors in the allocation of resources. We found a "yes" answer to both of these questions.

References

Bowen, H. R. *The Costs of Higher Education: How Much Do Colleges and Universities Spend Per Student and How Much Should They Spend?* San Francisco: Jossey-Bass, 1980.

Burke, J., and Serban, A. M. (eds.). *Performance Funding for Public Higher Education: Fad or Trend?* New Directions for Higher Education, no. 97. San Francisco: Jossey-Bass, 1998.

Choy, S. "Characteristics of Postsecondary Undergraduates." In *The Condition of Education 2002.* National Center for Education Statistics. [http://nces.ed.gov/pubs2002/2002025.pdf]. 2002.

Douglass, J. A. "A Tale of Two Universities of California: A Tour of Strategic Issues Past and Prospective." *Chronicle of the University of California,* Fall 2000, pp. 93–118.

Ewell, P. T. "Linking Performance Measures to Resource Allocation: Exploring Unmapped Terrain." *Quality in Higher Education,* 1999, 5(3), pp. 191–210.

Hovey, H. *State Funding for Higher Education: The Battle to Maintain Current Support.* San Jose, Calif.: National Center for Public Policy and Higher Education, 2000.

Jenny, H. H. *Cost Accounting in Higher Education.* Washington, D.C.: National Association of College and University Business Officers, 1996.

Jones, D. *Higher-Education Budgeting at the State Level: Concepts and Principles.* Boulder, Colo.: National Center for Higher Education Management Systems, 1984.

Lasher, W. F., and Greene, D. L. "College and University Budgeting: What Do We Know? What Do We Need to Know?" In M. B. Paulsen and J. C. Smart (eds.), *The Finance of Higher Education.* New York: Agathon Press, 2001.

National Center for Education Statistics. *Study of College Costs and Prices, 1988–89 to 1997–98.* Washington, D.C.: U.S. Department of Education, Office of Educational Research and Improvement, 2002.

U.S. Department of Education. *Instructions for the Integrated Postsecondary Education Data Surveys.* Washington, D.C.: U.S. Government Printing Office, 2002.

Wildavsky, A. *The Politics of the Budget Process.* (4th ed.) Glenview, Ill.: Scott, Foresman, 1998.

JANE V. WELLMAN *is a senior associate with the Institute for Higher Education Policy in Washington, D.C.*

8

Higher education systems in other developed nations that have operated without the student credit hour are increasingly interested in introducing it or similar metrics that facilitate internationalization of the curriculum and the introduction of more electives and student transfer options.

The Student Credit Hour: An International Exploration

Thomas R. Wolanin

This chapter explores if and how the credit hour is used in higher education outside of the United States. Its purpose is to discover if its use in non-U.S. settings holds lessons for U.S. higher education. The focus will be on its use in measuring student progress and attainment, with less attention given to its use for budgeting and other purposes. A systematic and global comparison of U.S. credit-hour practice with that of the rest of world is beyond the scope of this chapter. Instead, the focus will be on an exploration of how the credit hour is used in Europe because American higher education traces its roots to Europe and because American and European higher education are comparable in scale, sophistication, and complexity. The credit-hour experience in Australia and Japan will be more briefly surveyed.

The Credit Hour in the United States: A Brief Recap

As a point of departure for the international comparisons, I begin with a short recapitulation of how the credit hour is used in higher education in the United States. In U.S. higher education, particularly at the undergraduate level, the credit hour is a measure of students' academic progress and attainment based on a combination of time and achievement. The traditional formulation has been to award a student one hour or credit for one hour of clock time spent in class during a period of the academic calendar (for example, each week of a semester). It is assumed that some period of study outside of class accompanies each hour in class. Commonly, two hours outside of class is expected for each hour in class or a total of three hours per week per semester per credit hour. Full-time study is frequently defined as twelve credit hours or thirty-six hours of clock time per week of study (twelve hours in class and twenty-four hours outside of class), which is close to the U.S. full-time-employment norm of forty hours per week. Finally, credit is only awarded if a student meets the course achievement requirements (satisfactory performance on examinations, essays, laboratory, or internship evaluation).

Academic credentials (degrees, certificates, and the like) are generally awarded based on the accumulation of a set number of credit hours and a prescribed distribution of those credit hours (core, major, minor, lecture, lab, practicum, or internship). In some cases, institutions have additional credential requirements such as residency or time limits (the accumulation of credits in a particular place or within a limited time period).

The use of the credit hour enables students to have choices in constructing their academic program. They can usually select from a wide variety of combinations of courses to customize or tailor the program to their own interests as long as the total number of hours and their distribution meet the institution's credential requirements. The credit hour also lets students efficiently and flexibly spend their academic effort by allowing them to change programs or majors at the same institution without having to start from scratch where the program or major requirements are overlapping. Thus, the three hours' credit in calculus initially to be applied toward an engineering major can be subsequently applied toward an economics major if a three-hour calculus course is among the degree requirements for both majors. Similarly, students can more easily transfer between institutions that recognize the equivalency of each other's course work. That equivalency is usually assessed per course and credit hour.

In addition to measuring student academic progress and attainment, the credit hour is used to measure institutional and faculty workload and output for a large variety of budgetary and reporting purposes.

National Uses of the Credit Hour in Europe

More than forty nations in Europe have higher education institutions.[1] There is wide variation in their credit-hour practices. In a number of countries, particularly among the Nordics, academic programs are described in terms of credit hours that are similar to those used in higher education in the United States. In Finland, for example, "The length of the degree programmes is given in credits (*opintoviikko*, literally 'study week'). One credit is awarded for approximately 40 hours of work: lectures and other forms of instruction, exercises, seminars, and independent work at home or in the library. . . . The extent of the [bachelor's] degree is usually 120 credits" (European Commission, 1998; Ministry of Education, 2000, p. 35).

Sweden has a system of credit points (*poang*) in which the underlying assumption remains forty hours per week of academic work per credit per semester, and the bachelor's degree is 120 to 140 credit points (European Commission, 1998). The systems in Norway, the Netherlands, and Iceland are similar, with student workloads per semester measured in credit units (*vekttall*) in Norway, study points (*studiepunten*) in the Netherlands, and study credits (*namseiningar*) in Iceland (European Commission, 1998). In Iceland, however, where much of the academic year passes in darkness, the assumption is that full-time study is fifty hours per week of academic work, rather than the more typical forty hours.

French universities also use credits (*unite de valeur*) to measure the successful completion of a semester or year-long course in either compulsory or elective subjects, and many institutions of higher education in England have "modulized" their curriculum.

Other countries such as Germany and Portugal have only recently begun to organize their curriculum and degree requirements in terms of courses with credit-hour values. Finally, many nations such as Italy, Spain, and the formerly communist nations of eastern Europe and the Balkans maintain largely traditional systems.

In the traditional university systems, the time to the first degree tends to be longer (five or six years rather than three or four years) than in the United States, the curriculum is highly prescribed with little room for student choices or electives, and academic progress is measured by success on examinations. Several examinations may be the final and frequently the sole indicators of work done in a semester, comparable to final examinations in individual courses in the United States. Or examinations may punctuate the conclusion of all the work of an academic year, or half of a degree program (two or three years' worth of work). There may also be a final comprehensive examination at the conclusion of a degree program. Frequently, what would be considered a lecture course in the United States is not a unit of academic progress but simply one means to prepare for an examination. A student might have an academic plan culminating in the required examination(s) that included attendance at lectures, tutorials, and independent study. But it would be performance on the examination that mattered—not performance in any of the preparatory academic activities. Work toward a degree often culminates in a final research work or project (such as the *testi de laurea* in Italy or *Diplomarbeit* in Germany).

If there is a geographic pattern, the use of the credit hour seems furthest along in northwest Europe, especially Scandinavia, with its use diminishing as one moves south toward the Mediterranean. Higher education in the formerly communist countries of eastern Europe and the Balkans is the most traditional and makes the least use of the credit hour.

Higher education in Europe is overwhelmingly public, with a nonpublic or private sector that is small if it exists at all. Substantial control of higher education tends to be exercised by national government. Therefore, where the credit hour has been adopted, it is largely the result of national higher education reform legislation. Indeed, its use was one facet of such national legislation enacted in the first half of the 1990s in Finland, Sweden, Norway, the Netherlands, and France (European Commission, 1998). The general direction of change in national higher education systems in Europe is clearly toward an increasing use of the credit hour. However, this change is relatively recent where it is under way and incomplete even where it has been pursued most eagerly. Countries with traditional systems (such as Denmark) border those that have gone far down the credit-hour road (such as Sweden). Even within countries committed to the use of the credit hour, remnants of the traditional system remain. This juxtaposition throws into stark relief what is gained and what is lost by the transition from the traditional systems to the organization and measurement of academic progress and attainment by the credit hour.

The curriculum of traditional European institutions is largely faculty driven and determined. It tends to be prescriptive with little room for student choices or electives. A student is awarded an educational credential when the student has carried out the faculty's plan. The use of the credit hour reflects a curriculum that is more student-consumer or market driven. It facilitates student choices among a variety of course offerings, many of which are interchangeably useful and acceptable to meet various distribution requirements. Students are awarded an educational credential when they have carried out their own plans. The students' plans must, of course, fit within the faculty-determined degree requirements. However, these requirements are often broad and loose, and most important, they are constantly evolving in response to the market signals provided by student choices and preferences. In short, it can be argued that the credit hour is a witness to and facilitates the often-criticized curricular incoherence of American higher education, particularly at the undergraduate level. One scholar notes, for example, "The convenience of the credit hour as common currency has driven out the better but far less fungible currency of intellectual and curricular coherence" (Shoenberg, 2001, p. 2; see also Freeland, 2001; Kuh, 2001).

Having credit-hour practices alongside traditional ones also highlights an evolution in pedagogical philosophy. The traditional systems are organized around high-stakes tests (to use the American term). Systems based on the credit hour have more frequent assessments. The evaluation of student progress is more frequent and broken down into smaller units, such as three or four courses per semester, rather than the work of an entire semester or year. Indeed, the reality in a credit-hour system is that each course for which credit is awarded often has several assessments that are cumulated into a final course grade that determines whether credit should be awarded. Students receive more timely feedback on their progress, enabling them to make corrections and improvements as they move forward. In addition, these multiple and sometimes continuous assessments frequently employ a variety of measures of academic achievement, such as attendance, oral recitation, timed examinations, essays, research papers, and laboratory experiments. These several measures are more likely to recognize the multiple intelligences of students and their various learning styles. In sum, the credit hour is a key component of more educationally effective and efficient assessment systems because with it, assessments are more frequent rather than a single high-stakes exam, the assessments provide for more continuous feedback, and they are more sensitive to the variety of student learning styles.

Finally, credit-hour systems give students a great deal of flexibility in pursuing higher education. They can more easily transfer between majors or fields of study within the same institution or at multiple institutions. Students can more easily tailor their studies to fit their family, work, and financial needs. A greater variety of "nontraditional" students can be more easily accommodated in a credit-hour system. Adelman (1999) appropriately calls the path of higher education attainment in the credit-hour environment "portfolio building." In contrast, students in the traditional European systems are more like travelers following a path through a tunnel that has only a single exit. To change one's mind about the journey's destination requires starting over on a new journey rather than making a mid-course correction. The traditional system penalizes thoughtful and reasoned evolution in a student's educational plans. A credit-hour system indulges dilettantism and indecision. Curriculum coherence is in substantial measure the other side of the coin from student flexibility.

The trend in European countries generally toward the use of the credit hour can also be seen as one manifestation of the gradual democratization of European political and social institutions. Punctuated by the student "revolts" of 1968, European universities have become increasingly less authoritarian and more reflective of the interests and demands of student-consumers and other popular currents emanating from business, government, and the society at large. Meanwhile, democratization has continued apace in the United States with the absorption into the higher education mainstream of racial minorities, women, persons with disabilities, and older "nontraditional" students. These new groups have increasingly entered higher education in addition to the post-World War II massification of higher education, which opened it to a large number of students from all economic backgrounds. With a time lag of about twenty-five years later than in this country, higher education enrollments in Europe have also dramatically increased to accommodate a growing proportion of youth beyond secondary school and most recently to serve previously marginalized groups such as ethnic and racial minorities.

A major contrast between higher education in Europe and the United States is in the propensity of students to change courses of study within a single institution, to move around among institutions of higher education in a single country, and to pursue some or all of their higher education outside of their home country.

U.S. students are less likely to stay in the same major that they start with than their European counterparts. U.S. institutional practices vary substantially, with students frequently indicating only an interest or an intent about their major field for the first two undergraduate years and having substantial opportunities to change—even declaring a major in their third (junior) year. European students typically are admitted in effect into a major or a department at the beginning of their higher education. U.S. students are most likely to be admitted into a school or college (for example, liberal arts, education, or business) that offers a large variety of departments and majors. For European students to switch fields or majors is less common and more difficult than for U.S. students. One British scholar reported that only about 20 percent of English undergraduates change majors in the course of their undergraduate studies (Liz Thomas, Senior Research Fellow and Director of the Institute for Access Studies at Staffordshire University, oral communication, Oct. 29, 2001). Similarly, a study of student life in Germany reports that "one in five students change their study discipline and/or target degree" (Schnitzer, Isserstedt, Mussig-Trapp, and Schreiber, 1999, p. 24). A comparable percentage for U.S. students cannot be computed because no definite choice need be made until long into the higher education experience. However, if a comparable number in the United States can be imagined, it could well equal or exceed 100 percent, given how frequent and common changes of major are, particularly if the multiple changes by some students are counted separately.

U.S. students are also less likely to stay at the same institution that they start with than their European counterparts. Estimates for the percentage of students who change institutions while undergraduates in Britain and Germany were 3 percent and less than 10 percent, respectively (Liz Thomas, oral communication, 2001; Schnitzer, Isserstedt, Mussig-Trapp, and Schreiber, 1999). In the United States, on the other hand, an extraordinary 60 percent or more of undergraduates attend more than one institution of higher education (Adelman, 1999).

There is a chicken-and-egg aspect to interpreting the relative pervasiveness of the credit hour in the United States and Europe. Students in Europe transfer less often between majors and institutions than students in the United States because flexible credit-hour systems that would facilitate such transferring are less common. Or credit-hour systems are less common in Europe because students have less of an interest in switching majors or institutions. It can only be assumed that a rough equilibrium has evolved to match student demand for transferring with mechanisms (including the credit hour) to make the transferring possible within and between institutions in the same country.

Compared with the relative frequency with which European and American students study outside of their home country, the vagabond American student hopping between majors and institutions becomes the homebody. European students act, well, more European rather than German, French, or Finnish as they more often than American students undertake a portion of their studies outside of their home country. One recent study reports that about 3 percent of American students participate in study abroad during their undergraduate career whereas the rate is about 8 percent for European students (Hayward, 2000). Fully 41 percent of German upper-division undergraduate students report either having completed a study-related stay abroad or that they have plans to do so (Schnitzer, Isserstedt, Mussig-Trapp, and Schreiber, 1999). There are, of course, definitional issues about what constitutes study abroad. The central point is clear, however: European students are much more likely than American students to study abroad. In addition, most European students undertake their study abroad in another European country. This has encouraged and been encouraged by European institutions and arrangements that facilitate student mobility among European nations. Compared with the United States, this appears to be of more interest to Europeans than mobility between institutions in the same country or within a single institution. We now turn to these European institutions and arrangements to facilitate student mobility among European nations and the role of the credit hour in them.

Transnational Uses of the Credit Hour in Europe

The European Union (EU) has been the primary governmental institution promoting student mobility in Europe. Founded in 1951 as a six-nation organization focused on economic development, it has expanded both in its membership and functions. It now encompasses fifteen nations—Belgium, France, Germany, Italy, Luxemburg, and the Netherlands (1951); Denmark, Ireland, and United Kingdom (1973); Greece (1981); Spain and Portugal (1986); and Austria, Finland, and Sweden (1995)—and its functions include a mandate to "contribute to the development of quality education by encouraging cooperation between Member States" (Article 149 of the Treaty of Amsterdam, 1997). The EU describes its role in higher education as follows: "At the European level, education in general and higher education in particular are not subjects of a 'common European policy': competence for the content and the organization of studies remains at the national level" (European Commission, n.d., p. 1). In other words, the EU does not *govern* higher education but rather provides encouragement and a variety of incentives toward the goal of a "European knowledge society" (European Commission, 2001). Thus, the hallmark of European cooperative higher education activities is that they are *voluntary*.

Promoting student mobility—crossing national borders for higher education purposes—has been one of the most prominent and long-standing EU higher education activities. It first took institutional form with the creation in 1984 of the National Academic Recognition Information Centres (NARIC) network, "the purpose of which is to assist in promoting mobility of student. . . . by providing authoritative advice and information concerning academic recognition of diplomas and periods of study undertaken in other States" (European Commission, "NARIC," n.d.). These centers are typically agencies designated by national ministries of education. (A parallel and similar network has been established by the Council of Europe and UNESCO, the European Network of National Information Centres on Academic Recognition and Mobility [ENIC]. The two networks share a Web site: http://www.enic-naric.net.)

The major EU initiative was the establishment in 1987 of the European Action Scheme for the Mobility of University Students (ERASMUS) to respond to the difficulty faced by students in getting academic recognition at their home higher education institution for academic work done elsewhere in Europe. ERASMUS is headquartered in Brussels and supported by EU-appropriated funds. It is a cooperative network among institutions of higher education initially in EU countries. It has expanded to now encompass institutions in thirty countries. (Besides the fifteen EU nations listed earlier, it includes three countries of the European Economic Area [EEA]—Iceland, Liechtenstein, and Norway—and twelve "associated countries": Hungary, Czech Republic, Poland, Romania, Slovak Republic, Bulgaria, Estonia, Latvia, Lithuania, Slovenia, Malta, and Cyprus). Where the NARIC network assisted *individual* students to cross frontiers for higher education purposes, ERASMUS is a network of bilateral and multilateral agreements by which university *departments* agree to reciprocally accept the equivalency of academic work done by students. These cooperative projects range from two to thirty institutional partners and now involve about four thousand institutions of higher education in the thirty countries. These agreements are typically painstakingly negotiated on a course-by-course basis between departments.

The EU budget for ERASMUS is currently about $150 million per year. Additional funds are provided by national governments, institutions of higher education, and others. About 80 percent of the EU funds are used for grants to students who have applied to undertake a three- to twelve-month study outside of their home country. These grants, which are tailored to the individual student's needs, help cover the "mobility costs" of studying in another country, such as travel, language preparation, and cost-of-living differences. Students receive grants only if full academic recognition for the study abroad has been ensured in advance through ERASMUS. At least in principle, universities send and receive an equal number of students under the program.

An important evolution in ERASMUS came with the creation by the EU of SOCRATES in 1995. SOCRATES is an administrative umbrella for all of the EU education exchange and cooperation activities. These include language and faculty exchange programs, vocational training programs, and work-study at private businesses, many of which were modeled after or stimulated by ERASMUS.

With ERASMUS in 1995, the focus of EU's student-mobility action shifted from agreements between individual faculty and departments to agreements among *institutions,* more deeply involving university rectors in addition to faculty and department heads. Thus, the primary negotiating partners have evolved from individual students (through NARIC) to departments (through ERASMUS) and now to universities (through SOCRATES-ERASMUS). In addition, ERASMUS is now administered by the education and training staff of the EU. These administrators, rather than faculty members, have the primary responsibility for negotiating ERASMUS projects.

ERASMUS has been judged a success and has grown rapidly, reflecting its great popularity. The number of students applying for support always exceeds the number of slots available to be funded. Currently, about 100,000 students per year participate in ERASMUS projects, and more than 750,000 have taken part in it since its inception. A total of ten million students are eligible to participate in ERASMUS. About two-thirds of the annual flow of mobile students is organized through ERASMUS, with the remainder making other independent arrangements (Jallade, Gordon, and Lebeau, 1994–1995; Bollag, 1993, 1994, 1995a, 1995b; Desruisseaux, 1994).

Obviously, a key question for the effective operation of ERASMUS is how to measure and compare learning achievements for the purpose of transferring them from one institution to another. The initial approach for comparing academic activity at one institution with that at a second institution was to negotiate these relative values on a course-by-course or academic activity-by-activity basis among the faculty members at the respective institutions. As the size and scope of ERASMUS grew—encompassing a large number of students and institutions in the thirty countries—efforts began to develop a common metric.

In 1992 the European Credit Transfer System (ECTS) was launched as a six-year pilot program under ERASMUS, involving 145 higher education institutions and focusing on five subject areas: business administration, chemistry, history, mechanical engineering, and medicine. ECTS has steadily expanded beyond the pilot program to include more institutions and more subject areas. About one thousand institutions now participate in ECTS.

The common metric is "ECTS credits." The ECTS credit shares two basic characteristics with the credit hour in the United States. First, it is a measure of clock time spent on academic tasks. Second, it requires "passing" an academic assessment to receive the credits. To elaborate, quoting the program's literature,

ECTS credits are a value allocated to course units to describe the student workload required to complete them. They reflect the quantity of work each course requires in relation to the total quantity of work required to complete a full year of academic study at the institution, that is, lectures, practical work, seminars, private work—in the laboratory, library, or at home—and examinations or other assessment activities. In ECTS, 60 credits represent one year of study (in terms of workload). . . . ECTS credits are also allocated to practical placements and to thesis preparation. . . . ECTS credits are allocated to courses and are awarded to students who successfully complete those courses by passing the examinations or other assessments [European Commission, 1998].

Thus, for example, if a student spends three months abroad at a university that participates in ERASMUS and ECTS and passes a course that represents 20 percent of the academic work included in a full year of study at that institution, the student is awarded twelve ECTS credits ($0.2 \times 60 = 12$) at his or her home institution.

The family resemblance between ECTS credits and credit hours becomes even more striking when looking at the amount of academic work clock time that is assumed to equate to one credit. The *ECTS Users' Guide* provides the following example: "one institution may teach a 5-credit course unit as 24 lecture hours, 6 tutorial hours, and 60 hours of private study . . . whereas the other institution may teach the same 5-credit course unit in 24 lecture hours, 36 tutorial hours, and 30 hours of private study" (European Commission, 1998, p. 6). In other words, five ECTS credits equals ninety clock hours of academic work ($24 + 6 + 60 = 90$ or $24 + 36 + 30 = 90$). Continuing the arithmetic, one ECTS credit equals eighteen clock hours of academic work ($90 \div 5 = 18$) and a full year (sixty ECTS credits) equals 1,080 clock hours of academic work ($60 \times 18 = 1,080$). Finally, if we assume an academic year of thirty weeks, this works out to thirty-six clock hours of academic work per week ($1,080 \div 30 = 36$). This is identical to the number of clock hours of academic work for full-time study in the common credit-hour formulation described above, as well as being similar to the clock-hour assumptions that underlie the credit-hour systems in individual European nations, also described above. It is also noteworthy that the examples of ECTS credits are described as a mix of "contact hours" (in-class time) and noncontact hours (outside-of-class time). Finally, in the first example, the ratio of one contact hour to two noncontact hours is again identical to the most common credit-hour formulation in the United States.

In ECTS, institutions retain control of the requirements for the award of academic credentials (degrees), including the type of credits (introductory or advanced), the field in which credits are obtained, the sequence of courses through which credits are earned, and the concentration of credits by field (major, minor, or elective).

In 1999, the EU established a group to study the development of ECTS into a European Credit System (abbreviated EC[T]S), which would extend ECTS principles and practices to all higher education programs, not just those included in ERASMUS student mobility. The enthusiasts for and advocates on behalf of EC(T)S cite a number of basic advantages and benefits of such a system. The list of these advantages perhaps provides a useful perspective emphasizing the positives of the credit hour seen by Europeans. For them, the credit hour is the bright new future. In contrast, some Americans emphasize the negatives of the credit hour, viewing it as the stultifying heavy hand of the past. The European view of the advantages of the credit hour and the EC(T)S is as follows:

a. It increases transparency making it easier to understand and compare diverse educational systems.
b. It will improve recognition of academic and professional qualifications . . . resulting in increased employability throughout Europe.
c. It will provide the necessary flexibility to take into account the enormous range of study opportunities open to citizens in (Europe). . . . Credits allow bridges and links to be built between different modes and types of education. They help create multiple entry and exit points essential for lifelong learning.
d. It will facilitate regional, national, and international mobility. This mobility dramatically widens student study choices and EC(T)S provides the possibility for full recognition of studies taken abroad (credit transfer).
e. It also aids the recognition of the whole qualification thereby making it more portable and mobile. A major benefit of this system is that it includes credit transfer and credit accumulation and is available to all students—not just those on exchange programmes.
f. It facilitates collaboration between European institutions, e.g. the development of joint curricula, etc. [European Commission, "Extension," n.d., p. 3].

In sum, argue the advocates, "The advantages of adopting this framework are clear. . . . A majority of European countries have adopted credit systems of some type and the rest of the world is experiencing a similar 'credit revolution.' It is more difficult to understand qualifications and systems that are not credit-based" (European Commission, "Extension," p. 5). The advocates' vision is that EC(T)S could become the credit system in countries that do not have one, replace existing systems, or be the medium through which national credit systems become more comprehensible and useful for a variety of purposes. This would all occur in the context of a system that is voluntary and that maintains national and institutional autonomy.

The "Report for the European Commission: ECTS Extension Feasibility Project" (2000) recommended measured movement toward EC(T)S through a series of pilot projects primarily focused on facilitating the development of lifelong learning opportunities. It is clear, however, that many European nations and higher education institutions are not yet ready to staff the barricades of the "credit revolution" because they expressed reservations about possible threats to national and institutional autonomy and the risk that "à la carte" higher education will undermine curricular coherence.

Extending ECTS is part of a larger European effort known as the "Bologna process," which is aimed at developing a "European higher education area." This process takes its name from the 1999 Bologna Declaration in which thirty-one European ministers of education representing twenty-nine countries committed their governments to a ten-year program of higher education initiatives aimed at "greater compatibility and comparability of the systems of higher education." Achieving this goal is a key element in establishing "a more complete and far-reaching Europe."[2] The following are the six major objectives of the Bologna process:

Adoption of a system of easily readable and comparable degrees
Adoption of a system essentially based on two main cycles, that is, bachelor's degrees of three or four years and master's degree of one or two years rather than first higher education degrees of five or six years
Establishment of a system of credits, "such as in the ECTS system"
Promotion of mobility
Promotion of European cooperation in quality assurance
Promotion of the European dimensions of higher education—increasing "the development of modules, courses and curricula at all levels with 'European' content, orientation and organization." In other words, taking Europe to all students in addition to taking students to Europe (mobility).

Three observations can be made. First, increased use of credit-hour systems is seen as a key element in developing more integrated European higher education that, in turn, will make an important contribution to a more integrated Europe of the future. In short, decisions on whether and how to use the credit hour are important matters of public policy.

Second, the Bologna process can be seen as another step in the evolution of the locus of EU decision making about higher education. Through the Bologna process, national education *ministries* have been added as new major partners or interlocutors in developing EU education policy. Their activities and decisions have begun to eclipse in importance those taken by individual students (for example, NARIC), university faculty and departments (for example, ERASMUS), and university rectors (for example, SOCRATES-ERASMUS).

Third, the path of the future development of higher education governance in Europe can be imagined in broad terms in at least two ways. Along one route, it can evolve toward a situation comparable to that in the United States in which individual states (European nations) remain the primary decision makers and individual institutions of higher education remain substantially autonomous. In addition, cooperation and integration in terms of degree comparability, length of academic programs, the use of the credit hour, student mobility, quality assurance, and curriculum development would continue to develop but remain voluntary. The alternative future could be increasing governance of higher education by transnational institutions, most likely the EU in Brussels. The substantial historical, cultural, and linguistic differences among European nations argue for the first alternative. The European tradition of central-ized, *dirigiste* government, most visibly recently seen in the creation of the euro currency, suggests the second possibility. The tension between these two alternatives defines the basic elements of the debate over the implementation of the Bologna declaration and what lies beyond it for the governance of higher education in Europe.

Using the Credit Hour for Purposes Other Than Monitoring Students

Our discussion thus far has focused on the use of the credit hour to mea-sure the academic progress and attainment of students in Europe. In the United States, it is also used to measure institutional and faculty workload and output. Let us look briefly at its use in Europe for purposes other than monitoring students.

England has perhaps the most transparent system for awarding pub-lic funds from the national government to institutions of higher educa-tion, comparable to state support for public higher education in the United States. As in this country, multiple sources of funding are available for institutions of higher education. However, the largest share (38 per-cent) is awarded by the Higher Education Funding Council for England (HEFCE) (1998a). Of the funding from HEFCE, 70 percent is awarded by formula to support teaching. The annual grant to institutions is calculated by multiplying a base amount per full-time-equivalent (FTE) student times the number of students (Higher Education Funding Council for England, 1998b).[3] Students in clinical courses, laboratory-based subjects, and studio courses are weighted more heavily than all others. Premiums are also applied to some types of students (older and part-time and those studying in year-round courses) and for students at specialized institu-tions and at institutions in London on the assumption that there are extra costs associated with the education of these students or at these locations. The funds from HEFCE to support teaching are given as a block grant to each institution.

The key point is that in terms of national policy and the allocation of funds from the national government through HEFCE, the actual teaching effort of faculty (measured by credit hours or any other metric) does not appear. There may be some assumption about how much faculty effort it takes to educate base FTE students and how many such students are the norm for a faculty member to teach. However, these assumptions appear to be deeply buried because the amount per FTE student seems to be a his-torical number based on what institutions have spent over time in the past, rather than a normative number based on some notion of what institutions *should* spend to educate each FTE student. (On the other hand, almost all of the funding from HEFCE to support research at institutions of higher education is directly tied to the quantity and quality of research produced by faculty. The quality of research is measured by an elaborate periodic peer review process, the Research Assessment Exercise.)

If there is a general trend in government funding of institutions of higher education, it would appear to be the replacement of line-item budget with lump-sum or block grants from the government to the institutions. The goals are to give institutions more flexibility in managing their resources; to provide a simpler, more uniform and transparent system for allocating funds to institutions; and to build government policy priorities into the allocation formulas, which replace the line-item budgets. One policy priority is to relate funding to demand and outputs as measured, for example, by funding based on FTE enrollments.

The HEFCE funding formula for teaching is one example of such an FTE formula-driven block grant. Another example is the "taximeter system" for higher education finance in Denmark. The previous "micromanaged" line-item budgeting has been replaced with a block grant "based on the actual levels of pupil/student activity, objectively measured in full-time semesters or years" (Education Ministry, 2000, p. 1). In other words, grants to institutions are based on FTE enrollments. However, incentives to serve national priorities are built into the formula with twelve different rates for students enrolled in various courses of study. In the Education Ministry's frank words, there are "published annually in the government's finance bill . . . politically determined rates per unit of (student) activity, the regulation of which is a powerful tool to guide the supply of courses according to government priorities and policies" (Education Ministry, 2000, p. 1; see also Education Ministry, 2002).

Credit-hour systems permit the calculation of FTE enrollments for the purposes of these formulas, but the credit hour is not a precondition for these formulas. Indeed, Denmark is one of the countries that has proceeded least toward adopting the credit hour.

The Credit Hour in Japan and Australia

Having held U.S. credit-hour practices up to the mirror of credit hours in Europe, it may be worthwhile to look at U.S. practices in the light of higher education systems of developed non-European countries. The credit-hour experiences of Japan and Australia suggest themselves as potentially useful comparisons.

In Japan, much of the vocabulary of higher education rings familiar to U.S. ears, being the product of reforms adopted during the post-World War II occupation. The completion of an undergraduate degree normally requires that a student earn 124 credits during four years. The number of credits awarded is also related to time spent in class. Beyond this point, however, the Japanese system looks very different from its U.S. counterpart. Most undergraduate courses are two semesters (one year) long. They are typically taught by one ninety-minute lecture session per week with a single end-of-year examination. Such a course is worth one to four credits. (Given that some academic work is expected in addition to the time spent in lectures, the typical Japanese course expects roughly a similar amount of academic time spent by students per credit hour as that in the United States.) Therefore, to achieve thirty-one credits per year, students typically take ten, fifteen, or even twenty courses concurrently, particularly during the freshman and sophomore years.

More important, opportunities are extremely limited for students to change courses of study or majors, to transfer between institutions, or to stop out using the credits they have earned as easily negotiable academic currency. There are almost no flexible student choices and mobility within institutions, between institutions, and over time, based on the portability of academic credits. Despite the use of credit hours, overall the higher education system is highly centralized and regulated by the Ministry of Education. Even in areas where individual institutions enjoy some discretion, university administration tends to be rigidly bureaucratic.

In short, although many of the words of Japanese and American higher education are similar, the music is much different. The barriers to change and reform seem to be much higher in Japan. The presence or absence of credit hours seems to be largely irrelevant to that fact. The fundamental differences are cultural and political, deeply held attitudes about the appropriate pace and process for achieving change, and the relative value of achieving reform versus the cost in social harmony and disruption.

In Australia, individual university courses and degree requirements are denominated in credits. However, significant diversity exists among institutions in course-credit systems, including the terms used, the number of credits awarded per course, and the number of credits required for a degree. This lack of standardization is both a barrier to transfers between institutions and a reflection of the minimal demand by Australian students to transfer between institutions, particularly in comparison with U.S. students. Australian students also choose their majors early in their university studies and have a more prescriptive curriculum and fewer options in choosing their courses than U.S. students (Ministry of Education, Training and Youth Affairs, 2001; Karmel, 1999).

In both Japan and Australia, student choice and mobility are restricted, reflecting the limited implementation of U.S.-style credit hours. However, Australian higher education seems to be the antithesis of that of Japan in the level of innovation and change that has taken place. The number of students in Australia has increased dramatically beginning in the 1960s. In the 1980s, the structure of financing underwent a major overhaul, with the national government taking over primary responsibility from the states. At that time the Higher Education Contribution Scheme was introduced. It provides for cost-sharing or tuition charges to students. This "contribution" can be either paid at the time of enrollment (at a discount) or deferred and paid as an income-contingent surcharge to a student's income tax liability. Other examples of innovation include triennial budgeting, a sophisticated and aggressive effort to recruit foreign students, and the pursuit of strong government equity policy over the past decade to improve the participation of students from groups who are poorly represented in higher education, including students from low socioeconomic backgrounds, indigenous (aboriginal) students, students from non-English-speaking backgrounds, and students from rural or isolated backgrounds.

Conclusions

In the case of the increasingly widespread use of the credit hour in Europe (the "credit revolution"), its adoption is viewed as an important component of higher education reform. Its use has several important and salutary effects. As noted above, these include greater transparency of educational systems and credentials encouraging labor market and intellectual mobility, greater access to study opportunities for lifelong learning across Europe, and easier collaboration among European higher education institutions.

The use of the credit hour in Europe as well as in Japan and Australia generally follows the fundamentals of the U.S. model. In particular, these systems reflect the fundamental idea that it is a measure of academic effort that is measured in two ways: first, by time spent in academic activities, both in class and outside of class, and second, by successful performance or outcome—most often satisfactory performance on some type of examination.

In addition, the metrics of the U.S. credit hour appear to be common if not, indeed, universal. Specifically, full-time study is generally assumed to require in-class and outside-of-class academic work totaling thirty-six to fifty hours per week. Also, one unit of credit generally equals three hours of academic work per week per semester (about fifteen weeks).

The movement in Europe away from traditional organization of the curriculum in higher education toward an organization based on the credit hour places in stark relief the fundamental shift that this entails in who governs higher education. It marks an evolution from faculty-designed and -controlled curricular coherence (rigidity) toward student-determined curricular choice and flexibility (incoherence).

In the U.S. context, it is sometimes argued that the credit hour stifles innovation and reform. It is clear, however, that the absence of a credit-hour system does not automatically unleash the forces of innovation and reform in higher education. For example, the higher education systems of eastern Europe where the credit hour has made the least inroads are among the most stagnant and regressive in Europe. These systems have made the least progress in relating their curriculum to the labor market needs of a market economy or to the demands for relevance to cultures and languages of all who live in a given nation. They have also made the least progress in recognizing the democratic equity imperative, the expectation that higher education serves all people in society, regardless of their gender, ethnicity, race, religion, disability, or linguistic background.

On the other hand, examples of substantial innovation in higher education exist in the absence of the credit hour. Denmark's taximeter system annually recalibrates the economic incentives built into the institutional funding formula to link basic support for higher education to the achievement of the government's policy objectives. Australia aggressively pursues equity objectives. In both cases, the U.S.-style credit hour is not the norm.

The larger point is that the credit hour can either be a system that facilitates change and reform, as in much of Europe, or it can retard change and reform, as is arguably the case some places in the United States where it has become rigidly codified and bureaucratized. Whether change and reform occur is probably mostly related to broader social, cultural, economic, and political factors of far more weight and relevance than the credit hour. For example, the varying levels of student mobility among institutions and programs in the United States, Europe, Japan, and Australia are more likely related to basic cultural attitudes about what is appropriate in higher education than the presence or absence of the credit-hour system. In all of these places, students probably have about as much mobility as they want. (Of course, their "false consciousness" about how much they should want or how much would be good for them must be put aside.)

Among the factors that are perhaps most significant in determining the magnitude and pace of reform are the following:

The presence of labor market or social demand for change in the higher education system—that is, the demand for new goals for higher education

The availability of resources to implement change

Reform plans that make sense—that is, appropriate means to achieve new goals

Academic and political leadership and the will to transform public expectations into concrete actions

In comparison with these factors, the presence or absence of credit-hour systems are twigs tossed by the waves.

Notes

1. One would think that certitude about the number of nations in Europe with higher education institutions would be possible. However, as with many things that seem simple at first glance, the precise number depends on several things, such as, Do you consider Iceland and Turkey to be European nations? How do you deal with all the pieces of the former Yugoslavia? Should the higher education systems of Scotland, Wales, and Northern Ireland be considered separately from England? How should higher education in the constitutionally distinct ethnic and linguistic communities of Belgium and Switzerland be treated? What should be said about Cyprus, Vatican City, Andorra, Monaco, San Marino, and Liechtenstein? What constitutes a higher education institution? Rather than trying to settle all these questions, we will leave it at "more than forty."

2. The thirty-one ministers of education represented the thirty countries that participate in ERASMUS, with the exception of Liechtenstein and Cyprus and the addition of

Switzerland. Belgium and Germany were each represented by two ministers, one each for the Flemish and French communities in the case of Belgium, and one each for the national government and the Lander (states) in the case of Germany.

3. FTE is measured either in terms of the level of a student's enrollment measured in "credit points" compared with the number of credit points defined as full-time or by comparing the duration of the student's program with its duration if the student were attending full-time. Thus, if a student is in a program that will take the student six years to complete but that would be completed in three years of full-time study, the student counts as 0.5 FTE.

References

Adelman, C. *Answers in the Tool Box: Academic Intensity, Attendance Patterns, and Bachelor's Degree Attainment.* Washington, D.C.: Office of Education Research and Improvement, U.S. Department of Education, 1999.

Bollag, B. "Coordinating Academic Exchanges." *Chronicle of Higher Education,* Sept. 1, 1993.

Bollag, B. "Expanded Exchanges in European Union." *Chronicle of Higher Education,* May 25, 1994.

Bollag, B. "Final Approval Expected for 'Socrates' Program." *Chronicle of Higher Education,* Mar. 3, 1995a.

Bollag, B. "Former Communist States to Join European Union's Exchanges." *Chronicle of Higher Education,* Nov. 17, 1995b.

Desruisseaux, P. "Assessing Quality." *Chronicle of Higher Education,* Dec. 7, 1994.

Education Ministry. *Financing of Education in Denmark.* [http://www.uvm.dk/eng/publications/factsheets/taximeter.htm]. 2000.

Education Ministry. *Higher Education.* [http://www.uvm.dk/eng/publictions/factsheets/fact7.htm]. 2002.

European Commission. *European Credit Transfer System: ECTS Users' Guide.* Brussels, Belgium: European Commission, 1998.

European Commission. *Socrates-Erasmus: A Guide to Higher Education Systems and Qualifications in the EU and EEA Countries.* Luxembourg: Office for Official Publications of the European Communities. [http://www.europa.eu.int/comm/education/socrates/erasmus/guide/default.html]. 1998.

European Commission. "Report for the European Commission: ECTS Extension Feasibility Project." [http://www.europa.eu.int/comm/education/socrates/ectsrap.pdf]. 2000.

European Commission. "Higher Education in Europe." [http://europa.eu.int/comm/education/higher.html]. 2001.

European Commission. "European Credit Transfer System." [http://www.europa.eu.int/comm/education/socrates/ectsrap.pdf]. N.d.

European Commission. "European Credit Transfer System Extension: Questions and Answers." [http://www.europa.eu.int/comm/education/socrates/ectsfea.html]. N.d.

European Commission. "NARIC: Network of National Academic Recognition Information Centres in the Member States of the European Union, the Countries of the European Economic area and the Associated Countries in Central and Eastern Europe and Cyprus." [http://www.europa.eu.int/comm/education/socrates/agenar.html]. N.d.

Freeland, R. M. "Academic Change and Presidential Leadership." In P. G. Altbach, P. J. Gumport, and D. B. Johnstone (eds.), *In Defense of American Higher Education.* Baltimore, Md.: Johns Hopkins University Press, 2001.

Hayward, F. M. *Internationalization of U.S. Higher Education.* Washington, D.C.: American Council on Education, 2000.

Higher Education Funding Council for England. "Funding Higher Education in England: How the HEFCE Allocates Its Funds." [http://www.hefce.ac.uk/pubs/hefce/1998/98_67.htm]. 1998a.

Higher Education Funding Council for England. "Annex F: Student Load," In *Higher Education Students Early Statistics Survey 1998–99*. [http://www.hefce.ac.uk/pubs/hefce/1998/98_48.htm], 1998b.

Jallade, J.-P., Gordon, J., and Lebeau, N. *Socrates Programme: Higher Education (ERASMUS) Study Mobility Within the European Union: A Statistical Analysis*. European Institute of Education and Social Policy for DGXXII of the European Commission. [http://www.europa.eu.int/comm/education/socrates/erasmus/statisti;sum.html]. 1994–1995.

Karmel, T. *Financing Higher Education in Australia*. Canberra, Australia: Higher Education Division, Department of Education, Training and Youth Affairs, June 1999.

Kuh, G. D. "College Students Today: Why We Can't Leave Serendipity to Chance." In P. G. Altbach, P. J. Gumport, and D. B. Johnstone (eds.), *In Defense of American Higher Education*. Baltimore, Md.: Johns Hopkins University Press, 2001.

Ministry of Education. *Higher Education Policy in Finland*. Helsinki: Ministry of Education, 2000.

Ministry of Education, Training and Youth Affairs. *Higher Education Report for the 2001 to 2003 Triennium*. Canberra, Australia: Ministry of Education, Training and Youth Affairs, 2001.

Schnitzer, K., Isserstedt, W., Mussig-Trapp, P., and Schreiber, J. *Student Life in Germany: The Socio-Economic Picture*. Bonn: Bundesministerium Bildung, 1999.

Shoenberg, R. "'Why Do I Have to Take This Course?' or Credit Hours, Transfer, and Curricular Coherence." *General Education in an Age of Student Mobility*. Washington, D.C.: Association of American Colleges and Universities, 2001.

THOMAS R. WOLANIN is a senior associate at the Institute for Higher Education Policy in Washington, D.C.

The credit hour is a universal translator that allows complicated institutions to translate disparate activities into a common language. It contributes to bad habits within the academy, particularly in relation to goals and assessment of student learning. Further, ways need to be sought to correct for the inequities in the student credit-hour system.

The Credit Hour: The Tie That Binds

Jane V. Wellman, Thomas Ehrlich

This inquiry into the uses and definitions for the credit hour has been akin to the ancient tale about the blind men and the elephant.[1] Many different truths have emerged, and it is necessary to connect the pieces to find the shape of the whole. Here's what we learned:

• The credit hour is the metric that serves as common currency for an otherwise disparate system of higher education. The measure allows institutions to translate complex processes into readily understood public terms. It is the basis for student transfer, the primary building block for systems of public accountability (including enrollment monitoring, faculty workload, and budget allocation), and the means for translating learning into credentials. The credit hour is clearly not going to go away any time soon, nor should it.

• The history of the credit hour is a powerful story of a tool designed for another time—part of the move for efficiency early in the past century and inadequate (though not irrelevant) for higher education today. It is based on a mechanical system designed in an industrial era that awarded credits for time on task. A century later, we maintain the same accounting system.

• Despite a common folklore that ascribes certain meanings to the credit hour, there are no uniform or even consistent definitions for it. Like the laws in the Queen of Hearts' croquet court, it is often mandated but not defined (witness the role of the accrediting agencies regarding it). When the credit hour is defined (in appendices to data dictionaries that seem to be universally ignored), it continues to be as a measure of classroom time: one hour per week in class for fourteen or fifteen weeks equals one credit hour, twelve hours per week in class equals a full-time load, and 120 credit hours equal a baccalaureate degree. The metric is not justified in either learning goals or outcomes. It is also not consistently related to time or workload within institutions or between different types of institutions.

• The credit hour was initially designed to help standardize measures of high school work for college admissions at a time when fewer than 10 percent of high school graduates attended colleges. Now, it contributes to systemic disconnects between K–12 and higher education because it is the public signal about what counts and what matters in student achievement, a signal that is not related to either expectations for high school graduation requirements or skill levels needed to succeed in college. Whereas most institutions of higher education have long abandoned the fiction of equating credit hours with time on task, mandatory attendance laws clearly perpetuate time-based credit measures in high school.

• Our early supposition that the credit hour is a barrier to innovation in teaching and learning within higher education is only partially correct. One reason it does not necessarily or uniformly stifle innovation is that the measure is rarely audited within institutions or by external agencies—to ensure consistent enforcement once it is in place. Further, innovative institutions with a high degree of intentionality—those led by a group of individuals with a coherent vision of academic change and institutional reform—empower people to work around it. As a result, individuals who want to develop alternative measures of learning or to allocate resources on different terms can do so.

• At the same time, the metric of the credit hour perpetuates rather than causes some bad habits within the academy because it seems to measure learning through time and credit accumulation and not through learning goals or results. It contributes to the atomization of learning, caused by the high degree of student mobility within higher education and the fact that individual courses (recorded in units) have become individually fungible in the marketplace of degree production and do not have to be justified within a larger curriculum. The bachelor's degree is equated with the accumulation of 120 credit hours, whether or not the learning sequences make sense or add up to clearly defined learning results, and subject only to limited requirements involving course distribution and majors. If students obtain all of their course work from a single institution, they may have the benefit of a coherent and integrated curriculum. At the national level, however, only a few baccalaureate-degree recipients fall into this category because most students attend two or more institutions en route to their degrees.

• The credit hour has become embedded in regulatory systems throughout higher education in the United States. Although no single entity "owns" the credit hour, the federal government is its single biggest regulator. It was an American invention and until recently has not been used outside of the United States. Instead, we have found that countries that do not have the measure or some proxy of it typically have standardized, state-mandated curricula and a low degree of student mobility across institutions. The credit hour is increasingly being introduced in many of the western European countries and elsewhere, sometimes as a reform to promote curriculum flexibility and student mobility and sometimes as only a semantic gloss. The evidence from other countries helps to answer the question, If the credit hour did not exist, would we need to invent it? The answer seems to be yes.

• The budget incentive structures created by the credit hour reward accumulations of credits without regard to learning sequences. Thus, institutions have no fiscal incentive to reexamine curricula or to ensure that students pursue particular course sequences because they get paid for the credit hour no matter how they occur. Despite efforts to change state budget procedures, the dynamics of the budget process are one of the strongest perpetuators of the status quo within higher education. These dynamics favor the maintenance of base budgets as opposed to institutional change that risks resources (or loss of credit hours).

• In many states, the budget systems using the credit hour also favor research universities over comprehensive institutions or community colleges. Research universities typically have greater independence from government and as a result have latitude to define the terms of measurement to meet their institutional priorities. In addition, institutional cross-subsidies, for example, the redirection of resources from low- to high-cost areas, are masked in credit-hour-driven budgets. This dynamic works to the advantage of institutions with a mix of high- and low-cost programs, such as research universities, although it can perpetuate basic confusion about the real costs of any activity at any campus. The metric of the credit hour and its translation into measures of full- and part-time-ness also favor institutions that serve a high proportion of full-time students at the upper-division and graduate levels. Community colleges are at a particular disadvantage because they do not have the same opportunities for cross-subsidies as do research universities and they serve most part-time students, all at the lower-division level.

The key policy question for the study is whether the habits that have grown up around the credit hour are likely to change if the measure is altered. They could change in relatively modest ways from several actors that would cumulatively make a major difference. If the federal government, for instance, clearly said that credits are based on learning in the context of program goals, rather than in time, it would make a difference. The accrediting agencies could make an important change if they revisited their statements about credit units required for the degree and the basis on which they should be awarded. State funding agencies could think about ways to base budgets on head-count enrollments and sequences of courses or learning outcomes rather than on just counting credit hours.

External regulatory changes in the metrics, however, will not accomplish as much as changing internal institutional habits. The most important discussions about the credit hour need to occur within institutions, most of which seem to be operating on autopilot with respect to it. A good place to start might be with an internal institutional review of the ways that the institution has come to use the credit hour—for high school courses required for admission, to credits for degrees, to residency requirements for graduation, to faculty workload—to test whether, as currently employed, the measure can be justified under current institutional priorities. On most campuses, this inquiry will lead to small but significant revisions in the ways credit hours are used. The results will only strengthen higher education.

Note

1. This refers to an ancient Indian tale, in which six blind men are asked to each take hold of different parts of an elephant—the ear, the side, the trunk, the tusk, the tail, a leg—and to describe the animal based on what they could feel. Of course, not being able to see the whole animal, each comes up with a different animal.

JANE V. WELLMAN is a senior associate with the Institute for Higher Education Policy in Washington, D.C.

THOMAS EHRLICH is a senior scholar at the Carnegie Foundation for the Advancement of Teaching.

INDEX

Academic calendars, 10, 62–63, 64
Academic year, 75
Accreditation, 57–68; and academic calendars, 62–63, 64; credit hours defined for, 60–61, 63–64; federal regulation of agencies for, 77; national, 58–59, 63–64, 66–67, 68; purposes and role of, 57–58; regional, 58, 59, 60–63, 66, 67; specialized, 59, 60, 65–66, 67–68; standards for, 59–68; steps in process of, 58; for Western Governors University, 38–39, 61
Accreditation Board for Engineering and Technology, 65, 67
Accrediting Council for Continuing Education and Training, 59
Accrediting Council for Independent Schools and Colleges, 64
Adelman, C., 11, 103, 104
Advisory committee members, 3–4
Albert, L., 3
Alverno College, 31–32, 33, 35, 37, 46
American Association of Bible Colleges, 59
American Association of University Professors, 80
American Bar Association, 65–66, 68
American Federation of Teachers, 80
Articulation agreements, 39
Assessment, in Europe, 102–103
Association of Advanced Rabbinical and Talmudic Schools, 59
Association of American Colleges and Universities, 5
Association of Theologic Schools, 59
Australia, 113–114, 115

Baccalaureate degrees, requirements for, 62, 120
Barrow, C. W., 7, 8
Bollag, B., 107
"Bologna process," 109–110
Bowen, H. R., 87
Budgeting, 83–97; for community colleges, 87–88, 94–95, 121; dollar-based, 52; overview of process of,

84–86; performance-based, 92–93; program-planning budgeting system (PPBS) for, 10, 91; pros and cons of credit hour use in, 93–97, 121; for research universities, 95, 121; state systems for, 10, 86–93. *See also* Funding
Burke, J., 92

California State University (CSU): approach to faculty workload at, 51–53; Monterey Bay, instructional innovation at, 32, 33, 36
Capella University, 79
Carnegie, A., 7
The Carnegie Foundation for the Advancement of Teaching, 2, 5, 7–8
Carnegie units, 7–8, 88
Charter Oak State College, 11, 32, 34, 35
Choy, S., 93
City University of New York, 50
Classification of Instructional Programs (CIP) code, 16
Clock hours, 10, 75
Collective bargaining: faculty workload determined by, 51; innovation hindered by, 46, 55; and use of credit hour, 10–11; and weighted teaching units (WTUs), 52
College Entrance Examination Board of the Middle States and Maryland, 7
Colleges. *See* Community colleges; Institutions of higher education
Commission on Higher Learning, 61. *See also* North Central Commission on Higher Education
Common Data System, 10
Community colleges: budgeting for, 87–88, 94–95, 121; relationship between class time and credits awarded at, 23–28, 29–30
Community Colleges of Colorado, 79
Connecticut Distance Learning Consortium, 79
Cooke, M. L., 8
Council for Higher Education Accreditation, 77

Back Issue/Subscription Order Form

Copy or detach and send to:

Jossey-Bass, A Wiley Company, 989 Market Street, San Francisco CA 94103-1741

Call or fax toll-free: Phone 888-378-2537 6:30AM – 3PM PST; Fax 888-481-2665

Back Issues: Please send me the following issues at $27 each
(Important: please include series initials and issue number, such as HE114.)

_____

_____

_____

$ _____   Total for single issues

$ _____   SHIPPING CHARGES: SURFACE   Domestic   Canadian
                                   First Item $5.00 $6.00
                                   Each Add'l Item $3.00 $1.50
                 For next-day and second-day delivery rates, call the number listed above.

Subscriptions: Please __start __renew my subscription to *New Directions for Higher Education* for the year 2____at the following rate:

U.S.	__Individual $70	__Institutional $145
Canada	__Individual $70	__Institutional $185
All Others	__Individual $94	__Institutional $219
Online Subscription		__Institutional $145

**For more information about online subscriptions visit
www.interscience.wiley.com**

$ _____   Total single issues and subscriptions (Add appropriate sales tax
                 for your state for single issue orders. No sales tax for U.S.
                 subscriptions. Canadian residents, add GST for subscriptions and
                 single issues.)

__Payment enclosed (U.S. check or money order only)
__VISA __MC __AmEx # _____ Exp. Date _____

Signature _____ Day Phone _____
__ Bill Me (U.S. institutional orders only. Purchase order required.)

Purchase order # _____
                 Federal Tax ID13559302   **GST 89102 8052**

Name _____

Address _____

_____

Phone _____ E-mail _____

For more information about Jossey-Bass, visit our Web site at www.josseybass.com

PROMOTION CODE ND03

opportunities for native students and professors to work and study overseas, how to develop exchange programs, and how to help nonnative families adjust to U.S. culture. For those interested in how to internationalize higher education, this volume provides a wealth of practical advice.
ISBN: 0-7879-6290-2

HE116   **Understanding the Role of Academic and Student Affairs Collaboration in Creating a Successful Learning Environment**
Adrianna Kezar, Deborah J. Hirsh, Cathy Burack
Presents authentic models of collaboration that will help to develop successful student leaders for the next century. Argues that educators must show students by their own behavior that they believe in the power of collaboration, while still acknowledging that partnerships can be messy and frustrating. The topic of collaboration between academic and student affairs is now more important than ever if colleges and universities are to educate students for the new collaborative environment.
ISBN: 0-7879-5784-4

HE115   **Technology Leadership: Communication and Information Systems in Higher Education**
George R. Maughan
Decisions about investments in information system infrastructure are among the most important—and costly—decisions campus and system administrators make. A wide variety of needs must be accommodated: those of students, faculty, and administrators themselves. This volume will help mainstream administrators think through the decision making process.
ISBN: 0-7879-5783-6

HE114   **Developing and Implementing Service-Learning Programs**
Mark Canada, Bruce W. Speck
Examines service learning—education that brings together students, teachers, and community partners in ways that foster the student's responsible citizenship and promotes a lifelong involvement in civic and social issues.
ISBN: 0-7879-5782-8

HE113   **How Accreditation Influences Assessment**
James L. Ratcliff, Edward S. Lubinescu, Maureen A. Gaffney
Examples of working programs include new methods of distance-education program assessment, an institutional accreditation self-study at the University of Vermont, and the Urban Universities Portfolio Project.
ISBN: 0-7879-5436-5

HE112   **Understanding the Role of Public Policy Centers and Institutes in Fostering University-Government Partnerships**
Lynn H. Leverty, David R. Colburn
Examines innovative approaches to developing the structure of programs in both traditional academic environments and in applied research and training; attracting and rewarding faculty engaged in public service; and determining which policy issues to approach at institutional levels.
ISBN: 0-7879-5556-6

HE111 **Understanding the Work and Career Paths of Midlevel Administrators**
Linda K. Johnsrud, Vicki J. Rosser
Provides information to help institutions develop recruitment efforts to fill midlevel administration positions and enlighten individuals about career possibilities in midlevel administration.
ISBN: 0-7879-5435-7

HE110 **Moving Beyond the Gap Between Research and Practice in Higher Education**
Adrianna Kezar, Peter Eckel
Provides suggestions for overcoming the research-practice dichotomy, such as creating a learning community that involves all the stakeholders, and using campus reading groups to help practitioners engage with scholarship.
ISBN: 0-7879-5434-9

HE109 **Involving Commuter Students in Learning**
Barbara Jacoby
Provides ways to create communities that meet the needs of students who live off-campus—from building a sense of community within individual courses to the creative use of physical space, information technology, living-learning communities, and experiential education programs.
ISBN: 0-7879-5340-7

HE108 **Promising Practices in Recruitment, Remediation, and Retention**
Gerald H. Gaither
Identifies the best practices for recruitment, remediation, and retention, describing lessons learned from innovative and successful programs across the nation, and shows how to adapt these efforts to today's diverse populations and technological possibilities.
ISBN: 0-7879-4860-8

HE107 **Roles and Responsibilities of the Chief Financial Officer**
Lucie Lapovsky, Mary P. McKeoan-Moak
Offers strategies for balancing the operating and capital budgets, maximizing net enrollment revenues, containing costs, planning for the resource needs of technology, identifying and managing risks, and investing the endowment wisely.
ISBN: 0-7879-4859-4

HE106 **Best Practices in Higher Education Consortia: How Institutions Can Work Together**
Lawrence G. Dotolo, Jean T. Strandness
Gives detailed accounts of activities and programs that existing consortia have already refined, providing practical models that can be replicated or modified by other institutions, and describes how to start and sustain a consortium.
ISBN: 0-7879-4858-6

HE105 **Reconceptualizing the Collegiate Ideal**
J. Douglas Toma, Adrianna J. Kezar
Explores how administration, student affairs, and faculty can work together to redefine the collegiate ideal, incorporating the developmental needs of a diverse student body and the changes in higher education's delivery and purpose.
ISBN: 0-7879-4857-8

HE104   The Growing Use of Part-Time Faculty: Understanding the Causes and Effects
David W. Leslie
Presents analyses of the changes in academic work, in faculty careers, and in the economic conditions in higher education that are associated with the shift away from full-time academic jobs. Issues for research, policy, and practices are also discussed.
ISBN: 0-7879-4249-9

HE103   Enhancing Productivity: Administrative, Instructional, and Technological Strategies
James E. Groccia, Judith E. Miller
Presents a multi-faceted approach for enhancing productivity that emphasizes both cost-effectiveness and the importance of bringing together all segments of the educational economy—institutions, faculty, students, and society—to achieve long-term productivity gains.
ISBN: 0-7879-4248-0

HE102   Minority-Serving Institutions: Distinct Purposes, Common Goals
Jamie P. Merisotis, Colleen T. O'Brien
Serves as a primer on the growing group of minority-serving institutions, with the goal of educating leaders at mainstream institutions, analysts, and those at minority-serving institutions themselves about their distinct purposes and common goals.
ISBN: 0-7879-4246-4

HE101   The Experience of Being in Graduate School: An Exploration
Melissa S. Anderson
Addresses the graduate experience from the standpoint of the students themselves. Presents what students have reported about their experience through interviews, surveys, ongoing discussions, and autobiographies.
ISBN: 0-7879-4247-2

HE99   Rethinking the Dissertation Process: Tackling Personal and Institutional Obstacles
Lester F. Goodchild, Kathy E. Green, Elinor L. Katz, Raymond C. Kluever
Identifies the institutional patterns and support structures that enhance the dissertation process, and describes how the introduction of dissertation-stage financial support and workshops can quicken completion rates.
ISBN: 0-7879-9889-3

HE98   The Professional School Dean: Meeting the Leadership Challenges
Michael J. Austin, Frederick L. Ahearn, Richard A. English
Focuses on the demanding leadership roles assumed by deans of social work, law, engineering, nursing, and divinity, providing case illustrations that illuminate the deanship experience at other professional schools.
ISBN: 0-7879-9849-4

HE97   The University's Role in Economic Development: From Research to Outreach
James P. Pappas
Offers models the academy can use to foster the ability to harness the research and educational resources of higher education institutions as well as the potential of state and land-grant universities to provide direct services for local and regional economic development through outreach missions.
ISBN: 0-7879-9890-7

NEW DIRECTIONS FOR HIGHER EDUCATION
IS NOW AVAILABLE ONLINE AT WILEY INTERSCIENCE

What is Wiley InterScience?

Wiley InterScience is the dynamic online content service from John Wiley & Sons delivering the full text of over 300 leading scientific, technical, medical, and professional journals, plus major reference works, the acclaimed *Current Protocols* laboratory manuals, and even the full text of select Wiley print books online.

What are some special features of Wiley InterScience?

Wiley InterScience Alerts is a service that delivers table of contents via e-mail for any journal available on Wiley InterScience as soon as a new issue is published online.
Early View is Wiley's exclusive service presenting individual articles online as soon as they are ready, even before the release of the compiled print issue. These articles are complete, peer-reviewed, and citable.
CrossRef is the innovative multi-publisher reference linking system enabling readers to move seamlessly from a reference in a journal article to the cited publication, typically located on a different server and published by a different publisher.

How can I access Wiley InterScience?

Visit http://www.interscience.wiley.com

Guest Users can browse Wiley InterScience for unrestricted access to journal Tables of Contents and Article Abstracts, or use the powerful search engine.
Registered Users are provided with a *Personal Home Page* to store and manage customized alerts, searches, and links to favorite journals and articles. Additionally, Registered Users can view free Online Sample Issues and preview selected material from major reference works.
Licensed Customers are entitled to access full-text journal articles in PDF, with select journals also offering full-text HTML.

How do I become an Authorized User?

Authorized Users are individuals authorized by a paying Customer to have access to the journals in Wiley InterScience. For example, a university that subscribes to Wiley journals is considered to be the Customer. Faculty, staff and students authorized by the university to have access to those journals in Wiley InterScience are Authorized Users. Users should contact their Library for information on which Wiley journals they have access to in Wiley InterScience.

ASK YOUR INSTITUTION ABOUT WILEY INTERSCIENCE TODAY!